An Introduction to CNC Machining

AN INTRODUCTION TO
CNC MACHINING

David Gibbs

T.Eng., MIED
Senior Lecturer in the Department of Civil,
Mechanical and Production Engineering
Reading College of Technology

Cassell

Cassell Ltd: 1 St Anne's Road,
Eastbourne, East Sussex, BN21 3UN

British Library Cataloguing in Publication Data
Gibbs, D. A. W.
    An introduction to CNC machining.
    1. Machine-tools—Numerical control
    I. Title
    621.9′023   TJ1189

ISBN 0-304-31169-3

Photoset by Paston Press, Norwich
Printed and bound in Great Britain by Mackays of Chatham Ltd.

Last digit is print number: 9 8 7 6 5 4 3

CONTENTS

PREFACE

A prime objective of machine-tool designers right from the early days through to the present time has been the replacement of manual labour by devices providing for increased speed, accuracy and efficiency of production. Over the years there has been a steady rate of development, but without any radical changes in basic methods. Now, with the advent of electronics, and in particular the computer, we are witnessing changes that are completely revolutionising the metal-cutting trades. This is generally referred to as computerised numerical control.

It appears to many people that this revolution has taken place overnight, but this is not really the case, since the first numerically controlled machine was demonstrated in the USA as far back as 1945, while the first British machine appeared in 1952. Progress in the development and general application of the new technology was rather slow until the introduction of the microcomputer. Now the rate of change is gathering a momentum that appears unstoppable. Indeed, in writing a book dealing with the subject, being out of date before publication is a distinct possibility!

This is also a problem confronting people concerned with devising courses of study relating to numerical control, and the efforts of the City and Guilds of London Institute in introducing the 220 series of pilot schemes, first for setters and operators and later for programmers, are to be applauded. Likewise, the efforts of the many people up and down the country who have introduced college-devised BTEC units and more recently the standard unit at Higher Certificate level are worthy of praise. For, whatever strengths or weaknesses these courses may have, they form the foundation on which future progress will be built.

However, with such a rapidly changing technology changes in course structure are inevitable. Also, some people are beginning to question the approach to numerical control that treats it as a 'stand-alone' subject and argue for integration with existing manufacturing technology courses at all levels. Others question the emphasis that is often placed on programming, insisting that the more practical aspects, such as tooling, work holding and machine setting, are of equal importance, and that any worthwhile study of the subject must have a strong practical bias where programming is treated as a means to an end and not as the end itself. Arguments such as these will no doubt be given due consideration as courses are developed.

Because of the uncertainty this book has not been written with any particular course of study in mind, although it closely relates to the course requirements and practical bias of the City and Guilds schemes. It is hoped that the text will also be of value to BTEC students and to anyone taking a first-time interest in the subject. It is assumed that the reader will have at least a basic understanding of metal-cutting techniques and the related technology.

Any existing knowledge of manufacturing technology that the reader may have is likely to have been gained by the study and operation of conventional machines. It is because of this that the introductory chapter of this book makes a deliberate attempt to link the new technology with the old. This approach is further justified in that many machines currently in use are of conventional design but retrofitted with numerical control systems, and many of the training machines being acquired by educational establishments have design features that clearly establish the fact that they are updated versions of standard machines.

The wide variation in programming techniques makes any attempt to introduce the subject in a general way a rather difficult task. In including the exercises in Chapter 8 it has been assumed that the student will have assistance from the lecturer and that the peculiarities of whichever system is used will be fully explained. If the control system presented here is used, lecturers may be interested to know that copies of the program for each exercise can be obtained from the author via the publishers.

I wish to record my thanks to all the organisations and individuals within those organisations who supplied valuable information and the photographs included in the book. My thanks, too, are due to my technical editor, Chris Coyer, for his help and encouragement.

D. A. W. Gibbs
Wokingham 1984

ACKNOWLEDGEMENTS

The author and publisher would like to thank the following individuals and companies who kindly supplied photographs and other material for inclusion in this book:

Mark Enticknapp
Paul Lambert
Bridgeport Division of Textron Ltd
Cincinnati Milacron
Gridmaster Ltd
Hardinge Machine Tools Ltd
Mills Marketing Services Ltd
N.C. Engineering Ltd
P.G.M. Ballscrews Ltd
Softools GB
Stellram Ltd
R.H. Symonds Ltd
Tarex Berger Associates Ltd

Extracts from BS 3635: Part 1: 1972 are reproduced by permission of the British Standards Institution, 2 Park Street, London W1A 2BS, from whom complete copies of the document can be obtained.

1

AN INTRODUCTION TO THE CONCEPT OF NUMERICAL CONTROL

DEFINITION OF NUMERICAL CONTROL

'Numerical control' (NC) is the term used to describe the control of machine movements and various other functions by instructions expressed as a series of numbers and initiated via an electronic control system.

'Computerised numerical control' (CNC) is the term used when the control system includes a computer.

The two systems are shown diagrammatically in Figure 1.1. The control units may be free-standing or be built into the main structure of the machine. The operating panel of an integrated control unit is shown in Figure 1.2.

THE APPLICATION OF NUMERICAL CONTROL

Numerical control is applied to a wide range of manufacturing processes such as metal cutting, woodworking, welding, flame cutting and sheet metal forming. The text that follows is restricted to its application to common machine-shop engineering processes, namely, turning, milling and drilling, where it has been particularly successful.

THE ADVANTAGES OF NUMERICAL CONTROL

Numerical control is economical for mass, batch and in many cases single-item production. Many factors contribute to this economic viability, the most important of these being as follows:

(a) high productivity rates;
(b) uniformity of the product;
(c) reduced component rejection;
(d) reduced tooling costs;
(e) less operator involvement;
(f) complex shapes machined easily.

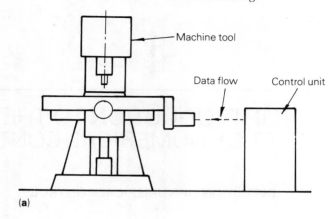

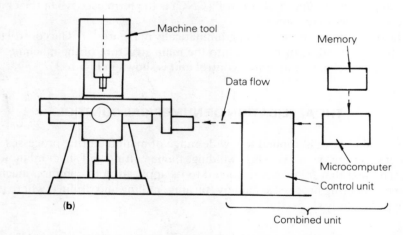

Figure 1.1 *Basic control systems* **(a)** *numerical control* **(b)** *computerised numerical control.*

It is also the case that fewer employees will be required as conventional machines are replaced by modern technology, but those that remain will of necessity be high-calibre technicians with considerable knowledge of metal-cutting methods, cutting speeds and feeds, work-holding and tool-setting techniques and who are familiar with the control systems and programming for numerical control.

THE CAPABILITY OF NUMERICAL CONTROL

The dramatic effect numerical control has already had on traditional engineering production techniques is now well appreciated. Machines controlled in this

Figure 1.2 *Integrated control unit.*

way are capable of working for many hours every day virtually unsupervised. They are readily adaptable to facilitate production of a wide range of components. Every function traditionally performed by the operator of a standard machine tool can be achieved via a numerical control machining program.

To appreciate just how versatile numerical control can be it is only necessary to examine very briefly the human involvement in the production of a simple component such as the one shown in Figure 1.3. The hole only is to be produced

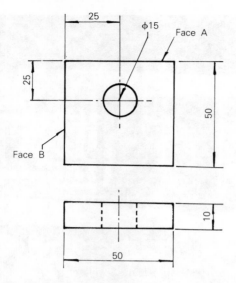

Figure 1.3 *Component detail.*

by slot drilling on a conventional vertical milling machine. The activities of the operator in producing the component would be as follows:

1. Select a suitable cutting tool.
2. Locate the cutting tool in the machine spindle.
3. Secure the cutting tool.
4. Locate the component in the work-holding device.
5. Clamp the component.
6. Establish a datum in relation to face A.
7. Determine the amount of slide movement required.
8. Determine the direction of slide movement required.
9. Move the slide, monitoring the movement by allowing for leadscrew backlash, slide friction, etc.
10. Lock the slide in position.
11. Establish a second datum in relation to face B.
12. Determine the amount of slide movement required.
13. Determine the direction of slide movement required.
14. Move the slide, monitoring the movement by allowing for leadscrew backlash, slide friction, etc.
15. Lock the slide in position.
16. Select a suitable spindle speed.
17. Determine the direction of spindle rotation.
18. Select a suitable feed rate.

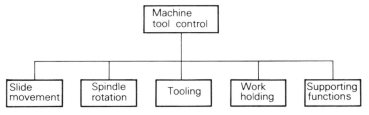

Figure 1.4 *Elements of machine control.*

19. Switch on the spindle motor.
20. Switch on the coolant supply motor.
21. Engage the feed and machine the hole.
22. Disengage feed and withdraw tool.
23. Switch off the coolant supply motor.
24. Switch off the spindle motor.
25. Remove the component.
26. Verify the accuracy of the machine movement by measuring the component.

From this list it can be seen that even the simplest of machining operations involves making a considerable number of decisions which influence the resulting physical activity. A skilled machinist operating a conventional machine makes such decisions and takes the necessary action almost without thinking. Nevertheless, the decisions *are* made and the action *is* taken.

It is not possible to remove the human involvement totally from a machining process. No automatic control system is yet capable of making a decision in the true sense of the word. Its capability is restricted to responding to a manually prepared program and it is during the preparation of the program that the decisions are made. Via that program the machine controller is fed with instructions that give effect to the decisions. In this way all the functions listed above, and many others not required in such a simple example of machining, may be automatically and repeatedly controlled. Figure 1.4 lists the elements of total machine control.

SLIDE MOVEMENT

The success of any manual machining exercise is dependent on many factors, not least of which is the experienced worker's practical skills. These skills are most in evidence when they affect the accuracy of the finished product, such as when they are involved in positioning, via the machine slides, the cutting tool and workpiece in the correct relationship to each other. This aspect of machining skill is also the crucial factor when the machine is electronically controlled.

Figure 1.5 **(a)** *Conventional centre lathe fitted with servo motors.*

Slide movement on numerically controlled machines is achieved by:

(a) hydraulically operated pistons;
(b) electric servo motors.

The use of electric motors is by far the most common technique. The motor is either directly coupled, or connected via a toothed belt drive, to the slide leadscrew. The servo motor, in effect, replaces the conventional handwheel and this is illustrated in Figure 1.5, which shows conventional machines, a centre lathe and a vertical milling machine, fitted with servo motors. A few machine designs have retained handwheels as an aid to setting or to provide for both numerical and manual control.

Machine tools have more than one slide and so the slide required to move will have to be identified. The plane in which movement can take place may be longitudinal, transverse or vertical. These planes are referred to as axes and are designated by the letters X, Y and Z, and sometimes W. Their location on common machine tools is shown in Figure 1.6. Note that the Z axis always relates to a sliding motion parallel to the spindle axis.

The direction in which a slide moves is achieved by the direction of rotation

Figure 1.5 **(b)** *Conventional milling machine fitted with servo motors.*

of the motor, either clockwise or counter-clockwise, and the movement would be designated as plus or minus in relation to a given datum. Figure 1.6 also shows how the direction of travel, as prescribed in BS 3635:1972, is designated on common machine tools. Slide movement and relative tool and work movement are discussed in more detail in Chapter 6.

The rate or speed at which slide movement takes place, expressed in metres per minute or millimetres per revolution of the machine spindle, will be proportional to the revolutions per minute of the servo motor; the higher the revolutions per minute the faster the rate of slide travel.

The length of slide movement is controlled by either the number of revolutions or the number of part revolutions the motor is permitted to make, one complete revolution being equal to the lead of the leadscrew, in the same way as one turn of a handwheel is equal to the lead of a leadscrew. In some cases there may be reduction pulleys between the motor and the leadscrew, as shown in Figure 1.7, in which case the linear movement obtained in relation to the motor revolutions would be proportionally reduced. The length of travel made, or required to be made, by a slide is referred to as a co-ordinate dimension.

Since the slide movement is caused by the servo motor, control of that motor

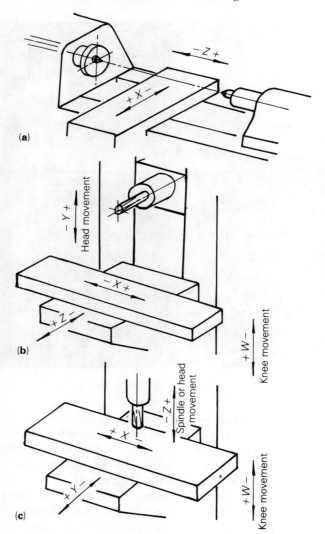

Figure 1.6 *Identification of slides and direction of the slide movement on common machine tools* **(a)** *centre lathe (turning centre)* **(b)** *horizontal milling machine (horizontal machining centre)* **(c)** *vertical milling machine (vertical machining centre).*

will in turn control the slide movement. The motor is controlled electronically via the machine control unit. All the relevant information, that is the axis, direction, feed rate and length of movement, has to be supplied to the control unit in an acceptable numerical form. The input of information to the machine controller is achieved in a variety of ways: perforated tape, magnetic tape, floppy disc and manually. Data input is covered in more detail in Chapter 5.

Figure 1.7 *Toothed belt drive from servo motor to leadscrew.*

Complex slide movements

So far consideration has been given to simple linear movement involving one slide. There are, however, many instances when two or more slides have to be moving at the same time. It is possible to produce a 45° angle as shown in Figure 1.8 by synchronising the slide movements in two axes, but to produce the 30° angle in Figure 1.9 would require a different rate of movement in each axis and this may be outside the scope of a simple NC system unless it is capable of accurately responding to two pre-calculated feed rates.

Similarly, the curve shown in Figure 1.10 would present problems, since ideally its production would require constantly changing feed rates in two axes. The curve could be designated by a series of co-ordinate dimensions as shown in Figure 1.11, and, providing the machine were capable of responding to the minute variations in size, a satisfactory result would be obtained, but the calculations necessary to approach the task in this way would be considerable. Complex slide movements such as that required to produce the curve can readily be achieved by the inclusion in the system of a computer capable of making the necessary calculations from the minimum of input data. Of course, the calculation of slide movements to produce complex profiles is not the only

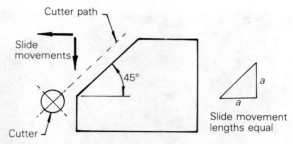

Figure 1.8 *Effect of equal rates of slide movement.*

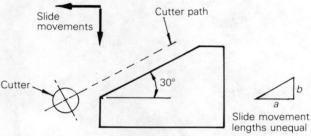

Figure 1.9 *Effect of unequal rates of slide movement.*

function of a computer. The other facilities it provides, in particular its ability to store data that can be used as and when required, will be considered later.

Verification of slide movement

An important function of the skilled worker operating a conventional machine is to monitor the slide movement and verify its accuracy by measuring the component. A similar facility is desirable on numerically controlled machines.

Control systems without a facility to verify slide movements are referred to as 'open-loop' systems, while those with the facility are called 'closed-loop' systems. A closed-loop system is shown diagrammatically in Figure 1.12.

The exact position of the slide is monitored by a transducer and the information is fed back to the control unit which in turn will, via the feed motor, make any necessary corrections.

In addition to positional feedback some machines are equipped with 'in-process measurement'. This consists of probes which touch the machined surface and respond to any unacceptable size variation. The data thus gathered are fed back to the control system and corrections to the slide movement are made automatically.

ROTARY MOVEMENTS

Sometimes the production of a component requires rotary movement in addition to the linear movement of the machine-tool slides. This movement is

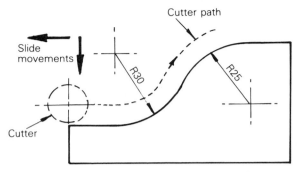

Figure 1.10 *Profile requiring constantly changing rates of slide movement*

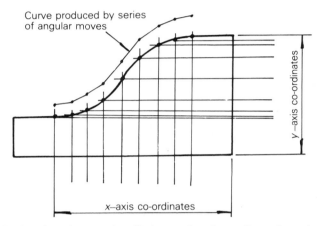

Figure 1.11 *Designation of a curved profile by a series of co-ordinate dimensions.*

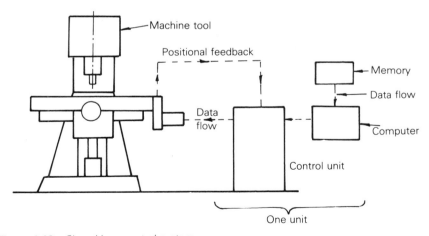

Figure 1.12 *Closed loop control system.*

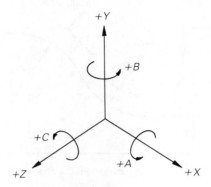

Figure 1.13　*Identification of rotary movements.*

provided by ancillary equipment such as rotary tables and indexers. These movements are controllable via the machining program. They are identified by the letters *A, B* and *C* as indicated in Figure 1.13.

CONTROL OF MACHINE SPINDLES

Machine spindles are driven directly or indirectly by electric motors. The degree of automatic control over this motion usually includes stopping and starting, and the direction and speed of rotation. Some very early systems, and perhaps one or two modern systems, do not include control of the spindle motions at all, switching on and off and gear selection being a totally manual operation. On the other hand, on some very modern control systems the torque necessary to carry out the machine operation can be monitored and compared with a predetermined value included in the machining program; when necessary the spindle speed will be varied automatically to provide optimum cutting conditions. (See 'Adaptive control', Chapter 9.)

The speed of the spindle is often infinitely variable, and will automatically change as cutting is taking place to maintain a programmed surface speed. Thus when facing the end of a bar as the tool nears the work centre the spindle speed will increase. In this way material removal is achieved at the fastest possible rate with due regard to tool life and the surface finish required.

The direction of spindle rotation required can be determined as follows:

1. Clockwise (CW). When the spindle rotates a right-handed screw would advance into the workpiece.
2. Counter-clockwise (CCW). When the spindle rotates a right-handed screw would retract from the workpiece.

CONTROL OF TOOLING

Numerically controlled machines may incorporate in their design turrets or magazines which hold a number of cutting tools. The machine controller can be programmed to cause indexing of the turret or magazine to present a new cutting tool to the work or to facilitate tool removal and replacement where automatic tool-changing devices are involved.

Simpler machines rely on manual intervention to effect tool changes. In these cases the control unit is programmed to stop the automatic sequence at the appropriate time and the operator will make the change. There is sometimes a connection between the control unit and the tool-storage facility and the correct tool to be used is indicated by an illuminated lamp.

Tooling is dealt with in more detail in Chapter 3.

CONTROL OF WORK HOLDING

Work holding is another aspect of numerically controlled machining that can include manual intervention or be totally automatic. The work-holding devices themselves can be fairly conventional: vices, chucks, collets and fixtures are all used. The numerical control can extend to loading the workpiece by the use of robots and securely clamping it by activating hydraulic or pneumatic clamping systems.

Again, as with tool changing, on simpler machines a programmed break in a machining cycle can facilitate manual intervention as and when required.

Work holding is dealt with in detail in Chapter 4.

SUPPORTING FUNCTIONS

The various supplementary functions a skilled worker would perform during a manually controlled machining operation are, of course, vital to the success of the operation. For example it may be necessary to clamp a slide, apply coolant, clear away swarf before locating a component, monitor the condition of tooling and so on. Slide clamping is usually hydraulic, and hydraulic pressure provided by an electrically driven pump with the fluid flow controlled by solenoid valves has long been a feature of machine tool design. With the new technology the control of the electrical elements of such a system is included in the machining program. Similarly, it is a simple matter to control the on–off switching of a coolant pump and the opening or closing of an air valve to supply a blast of cleaning air. Tool monitoring, however, is more complex and is the subject of much research and innovation ranging from monitoring the loads exerted on spindle motors to recording variations in the sound the cutting tool makes. Some of these more advanced features of numerical control are discussed further in Chapter 9.

QUESTIONS

1 Explain with the aid of a simple block diagram the difference between an NC and a CNC machining system.

2 State two advantages of CNC over NC control systems.

3 The common axes of slide movement are *X, Y* and *Z*. What is significant about the *Z* axis?

4 When is *W* used to identify an axis of slide movement?

5 What data are required to initiate a controlled slide movement?

6 On a vertical machining centre the downward movement of the spindle is designated as a *Z* minus. From a safety aspect this is significant. Why is this so?

7 How is an angular tool path achieved?

8 With the aid of simple block diagrams to show data flow, explain the difference between an open-loop and a closed-loop control system.

9 How would a manual tool change be accommodated in a machine program?

10 Explain what is meant by 'constant cutting speed' and how this is achieved on CNC machines.

2

MACHINE DESIGN

REPEATABILITY

The quality of conventional machine tools varies considerably. They are built to a price to meet a wide-ranging market. Generally speaking, the more expensive the machine is, the higher the quality of work that can be expected to be produced on it. However, an expensive conventional machine does not guarantee high-quality work. The key to success lies in the skills of the operator. The cheapest of machines is capable of producing very accurate work in the hands of the right person.

Skilled workers get to know their machines and make allowances for their failings. During the production of a component a skilled worker can, for example, compensate for leadscrew backlash, slide friction, lack of power, and so on. He or she can vary spindle speeds, feed rates and tooling arrangements. The approach to a final cut can be gradual until it is correct and before a final commitment is made.

With a numerically controlled machine tool responding to a predetermined program the capacity for readily varying the conditions when machining is under way is limited, and to make changes is inconvenient. As far as possible conditions have to be correctly determined at the time the program is produced and the machine set.

The slide movements are of prime importance. The movement must be precise and this precision must continue throughout a machining program which may involve thousands of components. The ability of the machine to produce continually accurate slide movement is called repeatability.

A precise definition of repeatability is as follows: 'the maximum difference which can occur between the shortest and longest positions achieved in a number of attempted moves to any programmed target position'.

Repeatability is expressed as the mean of a number of attempted moves. A typical figure for repeatability would be ±0.008 mm. It follows that some moves must be well within those figures.

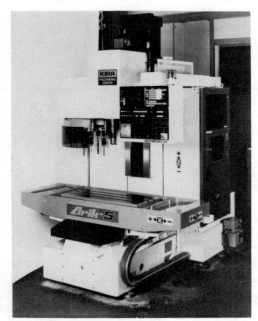

Figure 2.1 **(a)** *Vertical machining centre.*

Figure 2.1 **(b)** *Horizontal machining centre.*

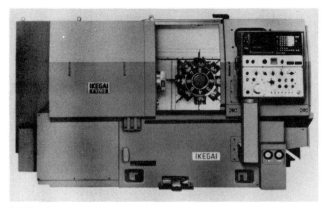

Figure 2.1 **(c)** *Turning centre.*

Repeatability is dependent on the following features being incorporated in the design of the machine;

(a) adequate strength;
(b) rigidity;
(c) minimum of vibration;
(d) dimensional stability;
(e) accurate control of the slide movements.

Although many conventional machines have been, and continue to be, converted to numerical control, such conversions being referred to as 'retrofits', their design in general does not meet the exacting requirements necessary to achieve a high standard of repeatability, while at the same time catering for the high rates of metal removal that modern tooling and electronic control have made possible. Radical changes in design were inevitable and have resulted in the machines now generally known as vertical machining centres, horizontal machining centres and turning centres. These are shown in Figure 2.1.

STATIC AND DYNAMIC LOADING

A simple analysis of the function of a machine tool reveals that it is subjected to certain loading which may be described as:

(a) static;
(b) dynamic.

Static loading is the term used to describe a situation where forces are acting on a structure when the machine, or that part of the machine, is not in motion. For example, due to its mass, a milling machine table exerts a static load on the

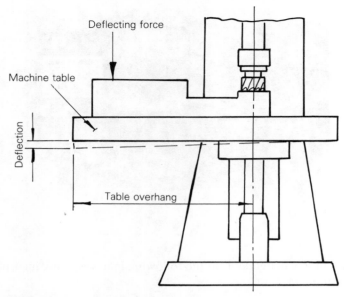

Figure 2.2 *Example of the possible effect of static loading.*

knee. If the table is offset on the knee that static load could cause the table to drop slightly at the unsupported end. A heavy workload would exacerbate the problem, which is illustrated in Figure 2.2.

Dynamic loading is the term used to describe a situation where forces are acting on a structure when movement is taking place. An example of this, shown in Figure 2.3, is the radial force exerted on a milling machine spindle as the cutter is fed into the work. The spindle could deflect.

Deflections such as those illustrated need only be quite small to affect the dimensional accuracy of the workpiece, so the machine structure and its sub-assemblies must be so designed to ensure that movement of this nature cannot occur.

BASIC STRUCTURE

For many years cast iron was considered to be the only material suitable for the basic structure of a machine tool. It possessed adequate strength and rigidity and tended to absorb vibration. In addition, the complex shapes required were easier to produce by casting than by any other method. Cast iron is still extensively used but its traditional position as the most suitable material is now challenged by steel and, more recently, by concrete.

When castings are used they are generally of one-piece box construction, heavily ribbed and stabilised by heat treatment.

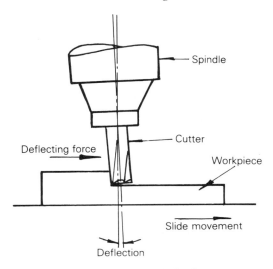

Figure 2.3 *Example of the possible effect of dynamic loading.*

Fabricated steel structures are increasingly being favoured for very large machines. Steel plates of the same thickness as a cast iron structure have approximately twice the strength. By reducing the plate thickness the weight of the structure can be considerably reduced, yet still provide the necessary strength. In use the rigidity of such structures has proved to be more than adequate. However, the general use of steel is limited by the problems of making complex shapes and by its resonant quality, which is not conducive to effective damping of vibration.

The use of concrete as a machine base is a comparatively new development. The advantages of concrete are its low cost and good damping characteristics. Very large structures can be cast on site, thus reducing the overall cost even further, since no transport is involved. Smaller structures can be provided with steel tubing cast into the concrete to permit easier handling. The cast iron bed of the machine is set on a cushion of air-setting resin and attached to the concrete by steel studs. The diagram in Figure 2.4 illustrates the concept. ·

MACHINE SPINDLES

The machine spindle is a very important design feature. The possibility of deflection has already been noted. In addition to the radial loads which cause deflection, a spindle assembly is also subjected to a thrust load acting along its axis. The design of the spindle assembly must be such that these loads are adequately contained. Inadequate support results not only in dimensional inaccuracies but also in poor surface finish and chatter. A well supported

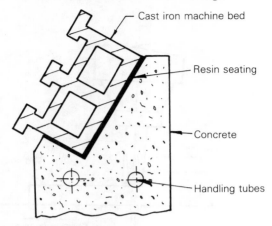

Figure 2.4 *Concrete base for a machine tool.*

spindle assembly is shown in Figure 2.5. Note that the spindle overhang has been kept to a minimum, a common feature of turning and horizontal machines.

The spindle of vertical machining centres presents additional problems, since it is a traditional feature of this type of machine for the spindle to move up and down. Obviously the more the spindle is extended the greater the risk of deflection. Some manufacturers have now moved away from the moving-spindle concept and instead the whole head assembly moves up and down.

Another unhelpful feature of vertical machining centres is that in order to

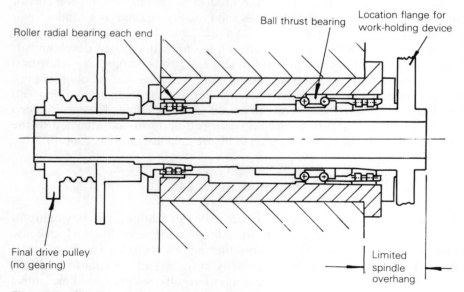

Figure 2.5 *Spindle assembly for turning centre.*

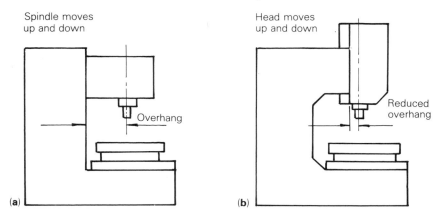

Spindle moves
up and down

Overhang

Head moves
up and down

Reduced
overhang

(a)   (b)

Figure 2.6 *Variations in the design of vertical machining centres* **(a)** *conventional design* **(b)** *improved design.*

provide an adequate work area the spindle head must overhang. The length of overhang must be kept to a minimum, and Figure 2.6 shows how one manufacturer has improved on the traditional design without reducing the work area.

The forces which cause deflection of the spindle also result in a tendency for the complete spindle-housing assembly to twist. This has resulted in an increased use of bifurcated or two-pillar structures where the spindle housing is located between two substantial slideways that reduce the possibility of twisting. A bifurcated structure is shown in Figure 2.7.

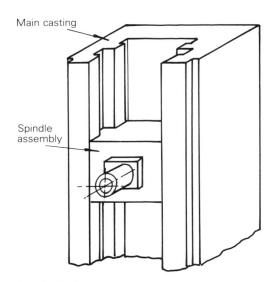

Main casting

Spindle
assembly

Figure 2.7 *Bifurcated structure.*

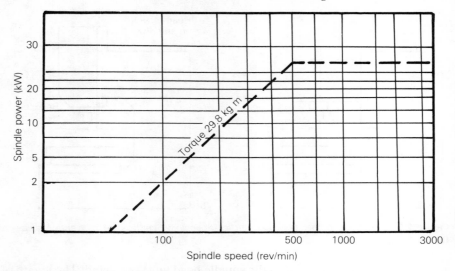

Figure 2.8 *An example of torque/spindle speed relationship when driven by a DC motor: constant torque after 500 rev/min.*

SPINDLE DRIVES

Two types of electric motors are used for spindle drives: direct current (DC) and alternating current (AC). They may be coupled direct to the spindle or via belts and/or gears. Many machines have a final belt drive which is quieter and produces less vibration than a geared drive.

The majority of modern machines use DC motors. By varying the voltage input their speeds are infinitely variable as they rotate and so a constant cutting speed can be maintained. The torque available from a DC motor is constant throughout most of the speed range, as illustrated in Figure 2.8.

There are some machines fitted with specially designed AC motors that also provide for variable spindle speeds, but the use of AC motors more usually involves a stepped drive, that is, a series of spindle speeds will be available and the selection of a particular speed may involve switching from one speed range to another, high or low for example, a feature that is common to many conventional machines. On numerically controlled machines the switching will be carried out as and when programmed via the control unit and may also include an automatic engagement or disengagement of an electrically operated clutch.

LEADSCREWS

The Acme form of leadscrew used on conventional machines has not proved to be satisfactory for numerically controlled machines. The movement of an Acme screw is dependent on there being clearance, i.e. backlash, between two

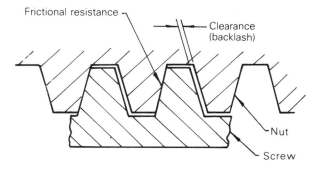

Figure 2.9 *Disadvantages of conventional Acme leadscrews.*

flanks. At the same time friction between the mating flanks of the screw means that considerable resistance to motion is present. These two disadvantages are illustrated in Figure 2.9.

Numerically controlled machines, except perhaps for a few cheaper training machines, are fitted with recirculating ballscrews which replace sliding motion with rolling motion, resulting in reduced frictional resistance. The balls, which in effect form the nut, recirculate in and out of the thread. The thread form is referred to as a Gothic arch and is illustrated in Figure 2.10. The balls make opposing point contact which virtually eliminates backlash. Figure 2.11 shows an external ball return and Figure 2.12 an internal return. The internal ball return is more compact.

The advantages of recirculating ball screws over Acme screws are:

(a) longer life;
(b) less wear;
(c) low frictional resistance;
(d) less drive power required due to reduced friction;
(e) higher traversing speeds can be used;
(f) no stick slip effect;
(g) more precise positioning over the total life of the machine.

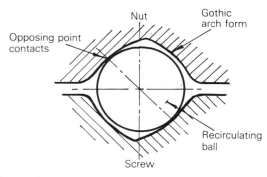

Figure 2.10 *Ball screw form.*

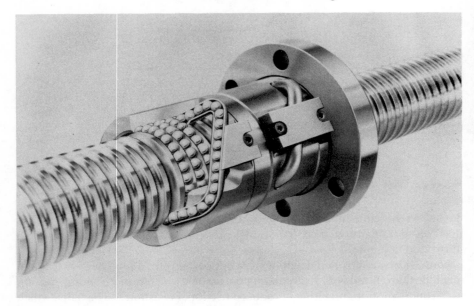

Figure 2.11   *Recirculating ball screw (external return).*

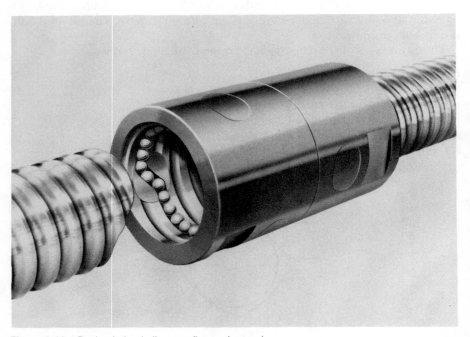

Figure 2.12   *Recirculating ball screw (internal return).*

Leadscrews are usually of substantial diameter and centrally positioned to avoid twisting the slide and thus reducing the efficiency of the movement.

MACHINE SLIDES

The movement of a machine slide must be smooth and responsive. There must be the minimum of frictional resistance to motion. In addition, wear, with its resulting dimensional inaccuracies, must be kept to a minimum.

The slides of a large number of numerically controlled machines have flat bearing surfaces. These surfaces are usually hardened and ground and coated with polytetrafluoroethylene (PTFE). This surface has a low coefficient of friction, is slightly porous and therefore is lubricant retaining. The load-bearing properties of flat surfaces are superior to those of other types of slides.

Where the machine loading permits, the sliding action of a flat bearing is sometimes replaced by a rolling action, in the form of balls or rollers, resulting in a marked reduction in the frictional resistance and requiring less power to achieve movement. Ball bushes, which may be circular or split, are illustrated in Figure 2.13. Figure 2.14 shows the practical application of split bushes. As motion takes place the balls recirculate. A similar slide arrangement involving recirculating rollers is illustrated in Figure 2.15.

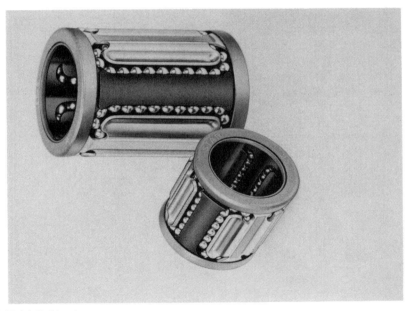

Figure 2.13 (a) *Ball bush.*

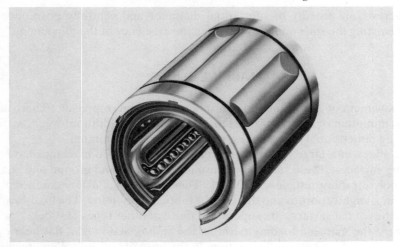

Figure 2.13 **(b)** *Split ball bush.*

Figure 2.14 *Application of split ball bushes.*

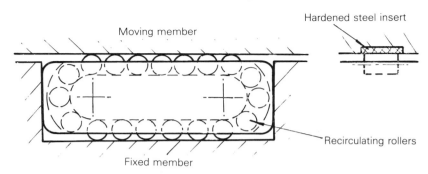

Figure 2.15 *Recirculating roller slide.*

Also used, but not very widely, are hydrostatic bearings where the bearing surfaces are always separated by oil or air supplied under pressure.

The forced lubrication of slides is common and protection is provided by telescopic or accordion covers.

SLIDE DRIVES

It was stated in Chapter 1 that both electric and hydraulic power are used to achieve slide motion. There are a number of very effective, responsive and thoroughly proved hydraulic systems currently in use, but by far the most common power source is the electric motor, and so the text will be confined to dealing only with this method.

Two types of DC motor are used:

(a) stepping motors;
(b) conventional, non-stepping motors.

Stepping motors are a special type of motor designed so that they rotate in sequential steps when energised by electrical pulses. A typical step would provide a slide movement of 0.01 mm. This type of motor was fitted to the earlier generation of machines but has now been largely superseded by the conventional type of motor, which in recent years has been the subject of much research, resulting in vastly improved designs which, together with improvements in control systems technology, make them much more responsive and easier to control than stepping motors.

The speeds of DC motors are infinitely variable. Constant torque is available throughout most of the speed range, which means that relatively small motors can be used, and when they are directly coupled to the machine leadscrew a torsionally stiff drive is provided. The motors provide regenerative braking, resulting in a virtually non-existent spindle overrun.

Considerable research is being carried out with AC servo motors. At present they are larger than DC motors providing equivalent power, and are also more costly. However, they need less maintenance and this is a factor very much in their favour.

POSITIONAL FEEDBACK

In Chapter 1 reference was made to the concept of open-loop and closed-loop slide positioning systems. The closed-loop positioning system is an important feature of any good numerically controlled machine. The concept can be summarised as: 'instruction–movement–information–confirmation'. The crucial feedback information is provided by a transducer.

A transducer can be described as a device which receives and transmits information. This information is received in one form, converted, and then transmitted in another form acceptable to the receiver.

A variety of transducers have been applied, with varying success, to numerically controlled machines. Two of the more common types are described below.

Rotary-type synchro

A rotary-type synchro transmits angular displacement as a voltage. Physically, this transducer is about 25 to 100 mm in diameter and 150 to 300 mm in length, being attached to one end of the leadscrew. Within this relatively small package there are a series of electrical windings. One of these windings, referred to as a rotor, rotates with the leadscrew. Around the periphery of the leadscrew are a series of interconnected windings which do not rotate and which are referred to as the stator.

The stator windings are fed with electrical power at a voltage rate that has been determined by the machine control unit in response to digital information relating to the required slide movement it has received via the part program. As the servo motor rotates the leadscrew, a voltage is induced in the rotor, and this voltage will vary according to the angular position of the leadscrew in relation to the stator windings. Information relating to the induced voltage is fed back to the control unit which, in effect, counts the number of complete revolutions and part revolutions the leadscrew has made, thus confirming that the movement achieved corresponds to the original instruction.

Optical gratings

An optical grating transducer transmits linear movement as a voltage signal in the form of a series of pulses.

The principle of the optical grating can be shown in a practical way as follows. Figure 2.16 represents a pair of optical gratings, each consisting of a number of evenly spaced parallel lines. One grating is fixed and the other is caused to move

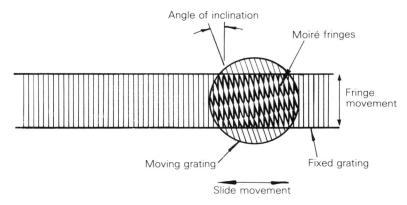

Figure 2.16 *Principle of optical grating.*

along. The reader is invited to reproduce the moving grating on either a piece of tracing paper or clear plastic film. Place the second grating over the first and, with the lines inclined at a slight angle, move the second grating across the first. A fringe pattern similar to the one shown will be observed moving across the fixed grating. This pattern is referred to as a moiré fringe.

There is a mathematical connection between the spacing of the gratings, the angle of inclination and the apparent fringe movement. This principle is applied to measuring the movement of machine slides.

For practical purposes the gratings are etched either on gelatine-coated glass or on stainless steel. The fixed grating is attached to the main casting of the machine and the moving grating is positioned immediately above the fixed grating, but is attached to the moving slide. Gratings for applications of this nature have 100 to 200 spacings per 25 mm.

If glass is used a light source is directed through the grating; if stainless steel is used the light is reflected off the surface. This light is focused onto a photo-transistor which responds to the fact that the projected light is uninter-rupted or interrupted, that is, a fringe is present or not present. The electrical pulses produced in this way each represent a known linear value. The number of pulses is counted and this information is fed back to the control unit as confirmation that the correct movement has been made.

Both the transducers described have a weakness. One monitors revolutions of the leadscrew, the other movements made by a slide. Neither of these factors may be a precise indication of the position of the tool in relation to the work, which would be the function of a perfect transducer. Such a transducer poses many design problems and has yet to be developed.

The locations of a linear and a rotary transducer on machine tools are illustrated in Figure 2.17.

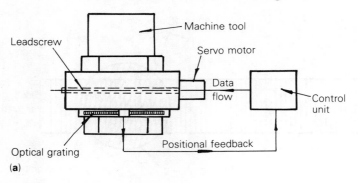

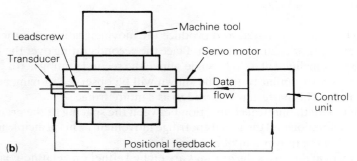

Figure 2.17 *Location of positional transducers on machining centres* **(a)** *linear transducer* **(b)** *rotary transducer.*

TEMPERATURE VARIATIONS WHICH AFFECT DIMENSIONAL STABILITY

Manufacturers design their machines so that the correct alignments are achieved at a stated temperature. 'Warm up' times are often quoted and sometimes warning lights are built into the control system. Deviation from the stated temperature can cause twisting or distortion of the machine castings and can have a considerable effect on the accuracy of the work produced.

Heat sources which have to be accommodated in the design of the machine, or otherwise eliminated, are as follows:

(a) heat due to friction in motors, bearings and slides;
(b) heat due to the metal-cutting action;
(c) heat due to accumulated swarf;
(d) heat in the environment.

Heat due to friction is eliminated or its effect reduced in a variety of ways. For example, main drive motors are sometimes placed outside the main structure

Figure 2.18 *Individual coolant supply to cutting tools.*

(which also helps to reduce vibration) and the final drive to the spindle is via belts. Motors which are attached to the machine body have heat radiation facilities in the form of vanes built into their structure. Some are cooled by a ducted air flow. Spindles may be air or oil cooled; sometimes when oil is used there are cooling facilities for the recirculating oil. Heat produced by slide movement is virtually eliminated by the efforts made to produce frictionless slides, as mentioned earlier.

Heat produced by the cutting action is kept to a minimum by ensuring that the correct cutting conditions prevail, that is, by using tools with the correct geometry for the material being cut and the operation being carried out, and by ensuring that the correct cutting speed and feed rates are employed. In addition, coolant, as a flood or as spray mist, can be applied to the cutting area. Some machines provide each cutting tool with an individual coolant supply, as illustrated in Figure 2.18.

Heat due to swarf accumulation can be a major problem, especially when the machines are totally enclosed for safety. The ideal situation is to have the swarf falling away from the machine. Figure 2.19(a) illustrates how the sloping bed of

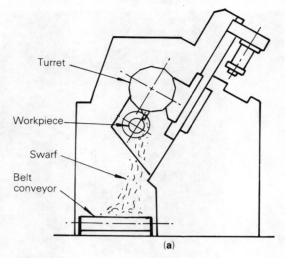

(a)

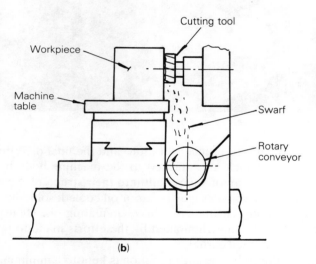

(b)

Figure 2.19 *Swarf removal arrangements* **(a)** *turning centre* **(b)** *horizontal machining centre.*

a turning centre permits the swarf to fall away, while Figure 2.19(b) shows a horizontal machining centre with the same facility. An added refinement is to have the swarf continuously removed by conveyor.

The room temperature for workshops containing numerically controlled machines should be maintained at a constant 20° centigrade. The presence of a radiator or a constantly opening and closing door can have a detrimental effect, and very warm summer days have been known to halt production in factories

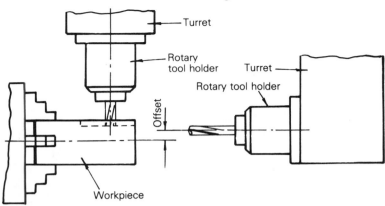

Figure 2.20 *Example of additional machining facilities on a turning centre.*

where the air conditioning was inadequate.

It is also worth noting that excesses in temperature not only affect the dimensional stability of a machine but can also cause malfunctioning of the electronic control systems.

ADDITIONAL MACHINING FACILITIES

A number of machines currently available have special design features that extend their capabilities by providing machining facilities not generally available. They include the following.

1. Turning centres with two turrets positioned in such a way that two tools can cut simultaneously. An example is shown in Figure 2.21.
2. Turning centres which use special tool holders that are power driven and can be programmed to rotate when the machine spindle is stationary, thus permitting the milling of flats, keyways and slots and the drilling of holes offset from the machine axis as illustrated in Figure 2.20.
3. A turning centre with a similar facility to that described above, but where the rotating holders are located in a separate turret. In addition the spindle, when clamped to prevent rotation, can be caused to slide in the Y axis, thus giving four-axis control: *X, Y, Z* and *C* (rotary).
4. A milling machine with two spindles providing for machining operations in the vertical and horizontal planes, a facility which is particularly useful and time saving when machining large components that cannot be readily reset. This feature is illustrated in Figure 2.22.
5. A turning centre using a tooling magazine, as opposed to a turret, to provide for a greatly extended tooling range.

Figure 2.21   Additional machining facilities provided by second turret.

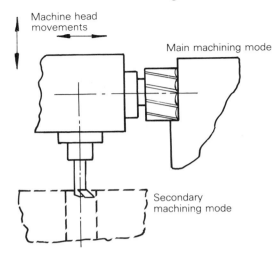

Machine head movements

Main machining mode

Secondary machining mode

Figure 2.22 *Example of additional machining facilities on a horizontal machining centre.*

SAFETY

The safety aspects of numerically controlled machines have to be related not only to the machine operator but also to the very costly equipment. There are two problem areas: the high voltage involved and the extreme mechanical forces resulting from high spindle speeds and rapid slide movements.

The electrical services are protected by lockable covers, and access should be limited to authorised persons.

The mechanical dangers are greatly reduced by total enclosure, a common feature of numerically controlled machines. This affords protection from flying swarf and broken tooling, reduces noise level and prevents contamination of the atmosphere by coolant, the latter being a considerable problem when spray cooling is employed.

When machines are not totally enclosed guards are used, these being fitted with interlocking switches so that there is no machine movement until the guard is correctly positioned.

The electrical control of mechanical features is also extended to work-holding devices. If the work is not correctly held there is no machine movement.

Excessive slide movement, which could damage the machine or workpiece, is prevented by limit switches, and this can also be extended further by programmable safety zones which fall into three categories: 'safe', 'warning' and 'fault'. Tool movement in the safe zone is unrestricted; in the warning zone it is only possible by the operator making a conscious response to a power cut-off; in the fault zone no movement at all is possible. The whole machine can, of course, be instantly immobilised by activating the obligatory emergency switch.

Reference was made earlier to conventional machines being retrofitted with numerical control systems. These machines often do not have the inbuilt safety features referred to above and because of this the utmost care must be taken in their use.

The reader should appreciate that, on all numerically controlled machines, whether purpose built or retrofitted, slide movements can be very rapid, and movements made at the wrong time or in the wrong direction can have disastrous results both for the operator and for the equipment. Accidents of this nature are more likely to happen during machine setting and program proving, and when re-starting after a program stop.

A clearly defined code of operation, with the accent on safety, is desirable for all remote controlled machine tools, particularly those used in educational and training establishments, and the student should be made fully aware of the inherent dangers.

QUESTIONS

1   Define 'repeatability' as applied to CNC machine tools.

2   List five qualities which need to be incorporated in a machine design if repeatability is to be maintained.

3   What are bifurcated structures and why are they used?

4   Why is it desirable that slide leadscrews should be centrally positioned?

5   What do you understand by the term 'dimensional stability' as applied to CNC machine tools?

6   List four factors which can affect the dimensional stability of a CNC machine tool.

7   Explain the difference between static and dynamic loading by quoting examples of where they occur in a CNC machine tool.

8   Why do some manufacturers recommend a 'warm up' period before a CNC machine tool is used?

9   How do some machine designs eliminate the problems caused by the heat present in swarf?

10   List the various techniques that are used on machine-tool slides to reduce the frictional resistance to motion.

11   List the advantages of using DC servo motors for slide movement on CNC machines.

12   Why is it that gearboxes are not necessary when machine spindles are driven by DC motors?

13   Why is the traditional Acme form of leadscrew unsuitable for CNC machines?

14   List the advantages of using recirculating ball screws to facilitate slide movement.

15   What is the name given to the thread form of ball screw?

16   What is a positional transducer and where and why it is used on a CNC machine?

17   What are the two problem areas that make safety an important consideration in the design of CNC machine tools?

18   Many CNC machines are totally enclosed. List three advantages of such an arrangement.

19   How can the danger of inadequate work holding be eliminated?

20   Explain the difference between 'safe', 'warning' and 'fault' safety zones and their purpose in CNC machine tool control systems.

3

TOOLING FOR NUMERICALLY CONTROLLED MACHINING

To the onlooker one of the most startling aspects of numerically controlled machining is the rapid metal-removal rates employed. That there are cutting tools capable of withstanding such treatment can seem quite incredible. Add to this indexing times of less than one second and automatic tool changing providing a 'chip-to-chip' time of around five seconds and it is easy to understand why many production engineers consider tooling to be the most fascinating aspect of numerically controlled machining.

MATERIALS FOR CUTTING TOOLS

Although high-speed steel (HSS) is used for small-diameter drills, taps, reamers, end mills and slot drills, the bulk of tooling for numerically controlled machining involves the use of cemented carbide.

The physical properties necessary in a cutting tool are hardness at the metal-cutting temperature, which can be as high as 600°C, and toughness. High-speed steel is tougher than cemented carbide but not so hard and, therefore, cannot be used at such high rates of metal removal. On the other hand, the lack of toughness of cemented carbide presents problems and this has meant that a tremendous amount of research has gone into developing carbide grades which, when adequately supported, are able to meet the requirements of modern machining techniques. It is only necessary to observe a numerically controlled machine in action to see how successful this research has been.

The hardness of cemented carbide is almost equal to that of diamond. It derives this hardness from its main constituent, tungsten carbide. In its pure form tungsten carbide is too brittle to be used as a cutting tool, so it is pulverised and mixed with cobalt.

The mixture of tungsten carbide and cobalt powder is pressed into the required shape and then sintered. The cobalt melts and binds the tungsten carbide grains into a dense, non-porous structure.

In addition to tungsten carbide, other hard materials such as titanium and tantalum carbides are used, and by providing tungsten carbide tools with a thin layer of titanium carbide, resistance to wear and useful life are increased by up to five times.

THE PRACTICAL APPLICATION OF CEMENTED CARBIDES

Solid tools
Solid carbide tools are somewhat restricted in their use owing to their lack of toughness. However, they are particularly useful when the work material is difficult to machine with high-speed steel, thus precluding the use of this material even for the small sizes referred to earlier. Solid carbide milling cutters as small as 1.5 mm diameter, drills as small as 0.4 mm diameter and reamers as small as 2.4 mm diameter are available. The successful application of solid carbide tooling depends greatly on the tool being short and mounted with the minimum of overhang, and the machines on which they are used being vibration free and having no play or misalignment. The correct speeds and feeds have to be determined with great care, often by experiment on the particular work in hand.

Brazed tips
As soon as the shank size of a cutting tool is large enough a more viable technique is to braze the carbide tip to a medium carbon steel shank. Drills, reamers, milling cutters and turning tools produced in this way are available.

Indexable inserts
While both the types of tooling referred to above have their particular uses, by far the most widely used application of cemented carbides is as inserts located in special holders or cartridges.

The advantages of inserts are as follows:

(a) correct cutting geometry;
(b) precise dimensions;
(c) no resharpening;
(d) rapid replacement.

The first two factors are particularly relevant where pre-set tooling is concerned. (Pre-set tooling is discussed later in the text.)

The inserts are indexable, that is, as a cutting edge becomes blunt the insert is moved to a new position to present a new edge to the work. The number of cutting edges available depends on the design of the insert.

The control of swarf is an essential requirement when high metal-removal rates are involved and this can be a built-in feature of the insert itself, in the form of a groove, or of the holder, in the form of a chip-breaking pad clamped on the top of the insert.

INTERNATIONAL SYSTEMS ORGANISATION CODES

Although there is still a wide range of cemented carbide grades, insert shapes and tool-holder designs currently available, the initially somewhat confusing situation was greatly helped by the introduction of International Systems Organisation (ISO) codes. Manufacturers' literature usually states where their particular products correspond with the ISO recommendations.

Carbide grades
Carbide grades vary according to their wear resistance and toughness. As the wear resistance increases the toughness decreases. The ISO code groups carbides according to their application and they are designated by the letters P, M and K and a number. A corresponding colour code of blue (P), yellow (M) and red (K) is also employed. An interpretation of the code is given in Figure 3.1.

Inserts
Inserts are designated according to shape, size, geometry, cutting direction, etc. An interpretation of the ISO code is given in Figure 3.2.

Holders and cartridges
Holders and cartridges are designated according to a number of factors which include tool style, method of holding the insert, tool height and width.

The shanks of the holders and cartridges can be 'qualified', that is, when the insert is located, the distance from the tool tip to a stated location face is guaranteed within a tolerance of ±0.08 mm. Qualified tooling and its application are dealt with in more detail later in this chapter.

An interpretation of the ISO code for tool holders and cartridges is given in Figure 3.3.

Figure 3.4 shows the four ISO-recommended methods of locating and clamping inserts in holders and cartridges.

THE PRACTICAL APPLICATION OF INDEXABLE CARBIDE INSERTS

Figure 3.5 shows how a variety of insert shapes may be applied to produce external and internal turned profiles, while Figure 3.6 shows a range of holders and inserts. Figures 3.7 and 3.8 show applications of inserts to milling operations. Figure 3.9 shows the application of cartridges to a face milling cutter body.

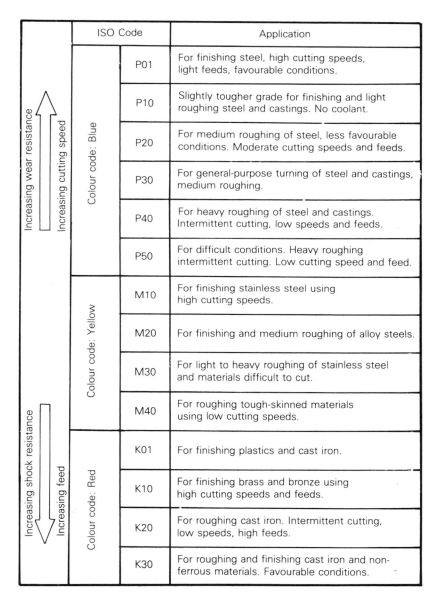

	ISO Code		Application
Increasing wear resistance / Increasing cutting speed	Colour code: Blue	P01	For finishing steel, high cutting speeds, light feeds, favourable conditions.
		P10	Slightly tougher grade for finishing and light roughing steel and castings. No coolant.
		P20	For medium roughing of steel, less favourable conditions. Moderate cutting speeds and feeds.
		P30	For general-purpose turning of steel and castings, medium roughing.
		P40	For heavy roughing of steel and castings. Intermittent cutting, low speeds and feeds.
		P50	For difficult conditions. Heavy roughing intermittent cutting. Low cutting speed and feed.
	Colour code: Yellow	M10	For finishing stainless steel using high cutting speeds.
		M20	For finishing and medium roughing of alloy steels.
		M30	For light to heavy roughing of stainless steel and materials difficult to cut.
		M40	For roughing tough-skinned materials using low cutting speeds.
Increasing shock resistance / Increasing feed	Colour code: Red	K01	For finishing plastics and cast iron.
		K10	For finishing brass and bronze using high cutting speeds and feeds.
		K20	For roughing cast iron. Intermittent cutting, low speeds, high feeds.
		K30	For roughing and finishing cast iron and non-ferrous materials. Favourable conditions.

Figure 3.1 *Selection of ISO carbide grades for metal-cutting applications.*

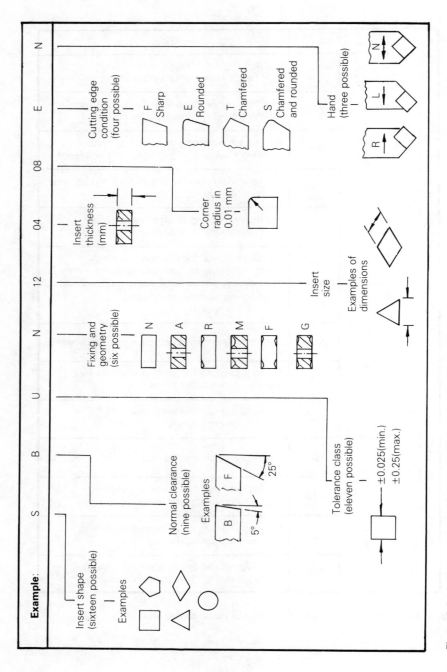

Figure 3.2 *Interpretation of ISO 1832 : 1977 designation of indexable inserts.*

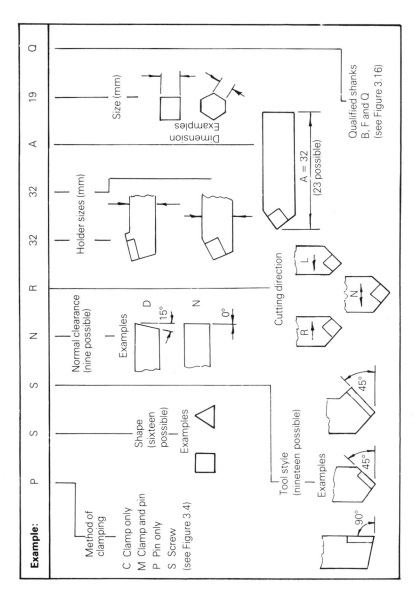

Figure 3.3 *Interpretation of ISO 1832:1977 designation of tool holders and cartridges.*

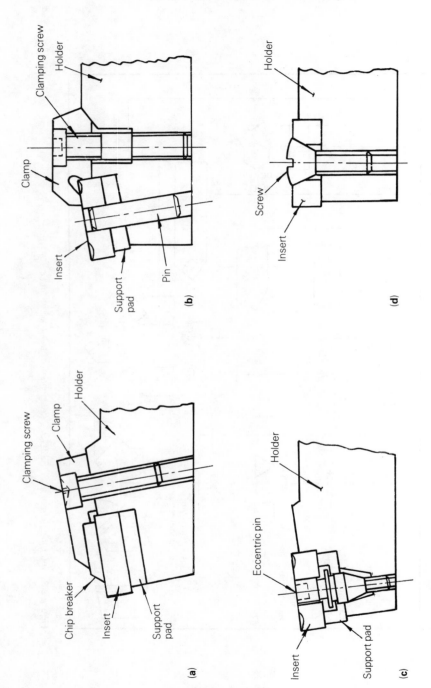

Figure 3.4 *Insert clamping arrangements* **(a)** *clamp only* **(b)** *clamp and pin* **(c)** *pin only* **(d)** *screw.*

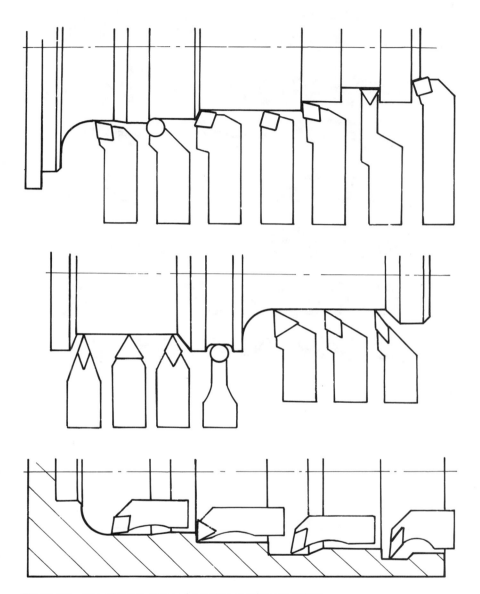

Figure 3.5 *Use of insert shapes for various turning operations.*

Figure 3.6 *Range of indexable insert turning tools.*

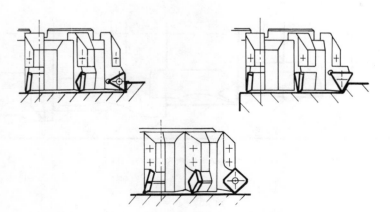

Figure 3.7 *Application of various insert shapes to face milling cutters.*

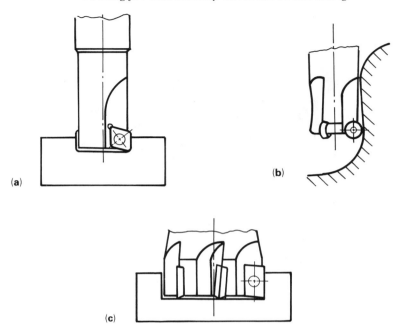

(a)

(b)

(c)

Figure 3.8 *Application of insert cutters to various milling operations* **(a)** *boring* **(b)** *contouring* **(c)** *slot milling.*

Figure 3.9 **(a)** *Application of cartridges to a face milling cutter.*

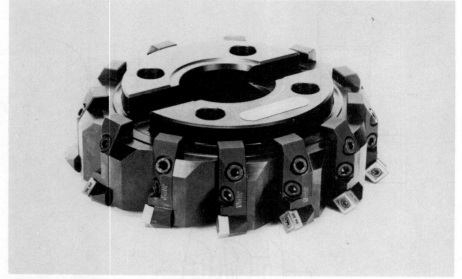

Figure 3.9 **(b)** *Application of cartridges to a face milling cutter.*

TOOLING SYSTEMS

The production of a machined component invariably involves the use of a variety of cutting tools, and the machine has to cater for their use. The way in which a range of cutting tools can be located and securely held in position is referred to as a tooling system and is usually an important feature of the machine tool manufacturers' advertising literature.

The tooling system for a machining centre is illustrated in Figure 3.10. Note the use of tool holders with standard tapers, a feature which can be very helpful in keeping tooling costs to a minimum.

The types of tool holders shown in Figure 3.10 are retained in and released from the machine spindle by a hydraulic device, an arrangement which lends itself to automation since it is relatively simple to control hydraulic systems using electrically activated solenoid valves which themselves can be controlled via the machine control system. The hydraulic force retaining the holder is supplemented by a mechanical force exerted by powerful disc springs, as illustrated in Figure 3.11.

Not all machines have automatic tool-changing arrangements and when manual tool changing is involved mechanical retaining devices are used. Conventional tool holders for milling situations use the tried and tested screwed drawbar arrangement, but unfortunately their use is not in keeping with modern machining techniques, where the accent is on speed. Because of this, several machine tool manufacturers have introduced tool holders of their

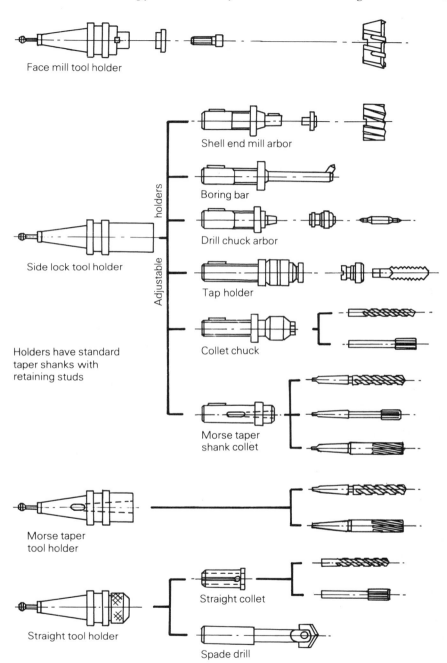

Face mill tool holder

Shell end mill arbor

Boring bar

Drill chuck arbor

Side lock tool holder

Tap holder

Collet chuck

Holders have standard
taper shanks with
retaining studs

Morse taper
shank collet

holders

Adjustable

Morse taper
tool holder

Straight collet

Straight tool holder

Spade drill

Figure 3.10   *Tooling system for a machining centre.*

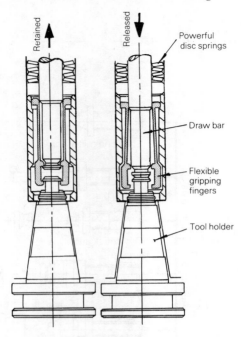

Figure 3.11   *Hydraulic–mechanical draw-bar assembly used on machining centres.*

own design which have dispensed with the need to undo a drawbar each time a tool holder is changed and as a result they have greatly speeded up the replacement process.

As with milling, a tooling system for a turning centre will indicate the range of tooling which can be accommodated on the machine. One such system is illustrated in Figure 3.12.

TOOL IDENTITY

The automatic selection and presentation of a cutting tool to the workpiece is a prime function of numerically controlled machining. To achieve this there must be a link between programming and machine setting. Tool stations are numbered according to the tooling stations available (see Figures 2.1 and 3.13), and when writing a program the programmer will provide each tool with a corresponding numerical identity, usually in the form of the letter T followed by two digits: T01, T02, T03 and so on. The machine setter will need to know the type of tool required and will set it in its allocated position. The transfer of information between the programmer and the machine setter is discussed in more detail in Chapter 8.

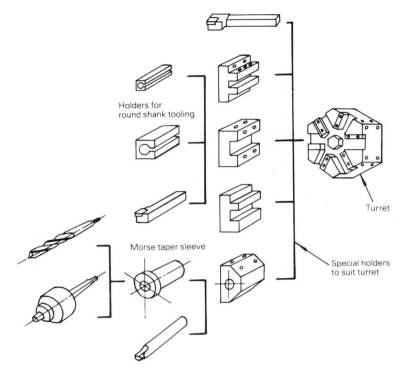

Holders for
round shank tooling

Morse taper sleeve

Turret

Special holders
to suit turret

Figure 3.12 *Tooling system for turning centre.*

INDEXABLE TURRETS

The turret is the part of some machines in which the cutting tools are located.
They are automatically indexable, that is, they can be programmed to rotate to
a new position so that a different tool can be presented to the work. Indexable
turrets are used on the majority of turning centres and on some milling/drilling
machines.

There are a number of turret configurations currently available on turning
centres. Several different types appear in the illustrations used throughout this
book. The number of tools which can be accommodated varies with machine
type, but eight or ten tool positions are usually sufficient to satisfy most
machining requirements, and in many cases a standard set-up consisting of a
range of external and internal turning tools is advised.

There are some machines in which the turret is removable and, if two turrets
are available, the spare one can be loaded with tools for a particular job before
they are needed and then the turret is attached to the machine when required,
a technique which reduces the machine down time considerably.

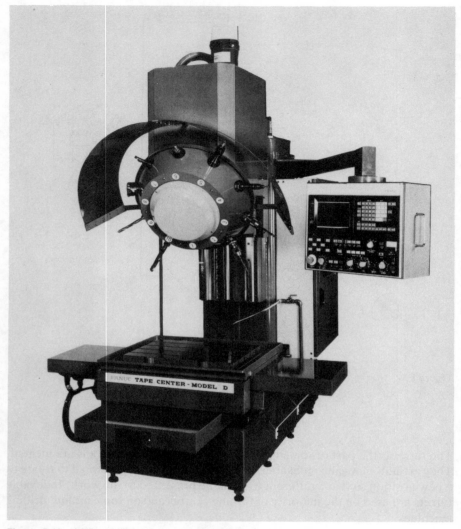

Figure 3.13 *Milling/drilling centre with indexable turret.*

A variation of the rotating turret is the indexable slide on which the tools are mounted. The manufacturers of this particular arrangement claim that linear tool indexing is much more rapid than rotary indexing. An optional extra available is a sub base plate to which the tools may be attached away from the machine. As with the removable turret referred to above, this base plate is interchangeable and so a spare one can be loaded with tools in advance and then quickly attached to the machine when required.

Turrets generally fitted to milling/drilling machines are somewhat different from those fitted to turning centres, because each tooling position is in fact a spindle which has to rotate at a predetermined speed. Only the tool in the machining position will rotate, the others remaining stationary. A turret of this type, with ten tooling positions, is shown in Figure 3.13. (The concept of individually rotating tool holders has been extended more recently to turning centres. See Chapter 2.)

TOOL MAGAZINES

A tool magazine is an indexable storage facility used on machining centres to store tools not in use. The two most common types of magazines are the rotary drum type illustrated in Figure 2.1(a)–(b) and the chain type illustrated in Figure 3.14. When a tool is called into use the magazine will index, on most machines by the shortest route, to bring the tool to a position where it is accessible to a mechanical handling device. When the tool is no longer required it is returned to its allotted position in the magazine prior to the magazine indexing to the next tool called.

The position of the tool magazine in relation to the spindle varies from one

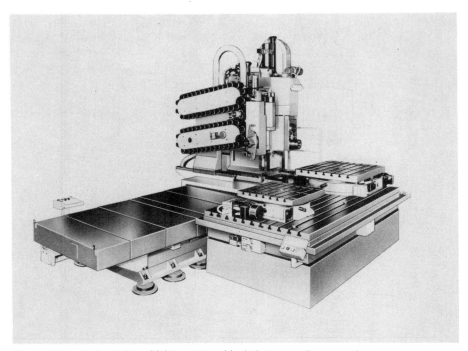

Figure 3.14 *Horizontal machining centre with chain-type tooling magazines.*

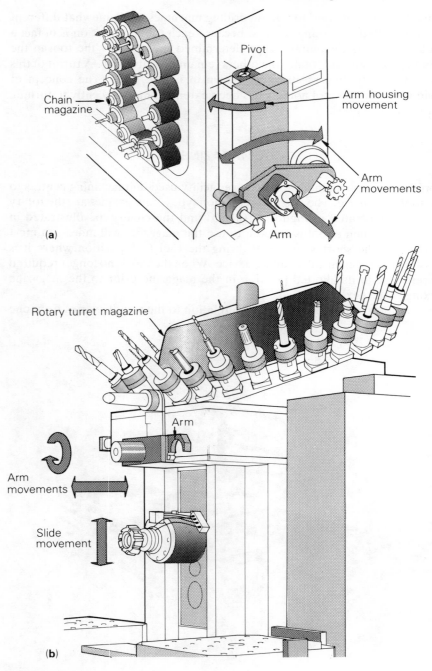

Figure 3.15 *Auto tool changers.*

machine to another. There are also variations in the design of the tool-handling devices. The two features are, of course, interrelated. Two arrangements are shown in Figure 3.15.

The capacity of magazines is another variable feature, with 12 to 24 stations being typical numbers for the rotary drum magazines and anything from 24 to 180 for the chain type.

REPLACEMENT TOOLING

From time to time, owing to wear or breakage, cutting tools have to be replaced. Such changes need to be rapid, with the minimum loss of machining time.

If the machining program is to remain valid, one of two requirements must be met:

1. The replacement tool must be identical to the original.
2. The program must be capable of temporary modification to accommodate the tool variations.

Identical replacement tooling can be achieved by using qualified or pre-set tooling. Temporary program modifications are achieved by offsetting the tool from its original datum.

QUALIFIED TOOLING

The ISO code illustrated in Figure 3.3 refers to qualified tooling. The dimensions from up to three datum faces to the tool tip can be guaranteed within ±0.08 mm. Thus if the tolerance on the dimension being machined is such that a variation in size within ±0.08 mm is acceptable, one tool can readily be replaced by another. Precise location of the holder or cartridge in the machine turret or spindle is, of course, an essential feature of replacing tooling of this type. The qualified dimensions are illustrated in Figure 3.16.

PRE-SET TOOLING

Pre-set tooling involves setting the cutting edge of the tool in relation to a datum face to predetermined dimensions, these dimensions having been taken into consideration when the part program was written. A simple explanation of pre-setting is given in Figure 3.17. The through hole in the component is produced by drilling, and drill A is to be replaced by drill B. Since the depth of travel on a through hole is not precise, it would be sufficient to set the projecting length of the drill with a rule and, providing dimension X is the same for the replacement drill as it was for the original, the program would still be valid.

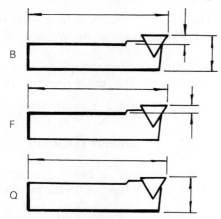

Figure 3.16 *Qualified tooling. Dimensions indicated guaranteed to within ±0.08 mm.*

When closer tolerances are involved the setting technique will need to be more precise. A wide range of specialised equipment is commercially available, the basic requirements of such equipment being a dummy tool locating/holding device with datum faces and appropriate measuring instruments. The tip of the tool is then set to predetermined dimensions in relation to datums as illustrated in Figure 3.18.

The more elaborate tool-setting equipment uses optical projection. An example is shown in Figure 3.19.

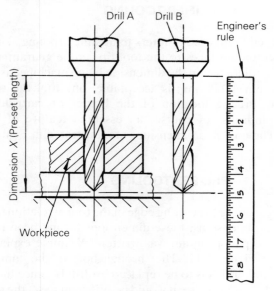

Figure 3.17 *Simple pre-setting of tool length.*

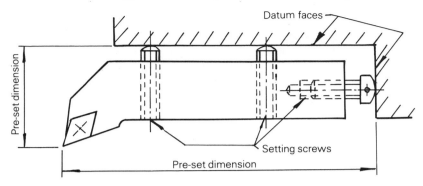

Figure 3.18 *Principle of pre-setting a tool holder.*

CUTTER COMPENSATION

The basis of numerical control is programming machine slide movements to occur over a stated distance in relation to a predetermined datum. Generally there is one datum for each axis of movement. However, most machining operations involve the use of more than one tool, varying in length or diameter, which means that if the cutting edge of one tool is set to the datum to which slide movements are to be related, tools which have dimensional variations from the set tool will not start their movements from the same datum. Some compensation in slide movement is necessary to accommodate the dimensional variations of the tools. This compensation is referred to as tool offset and the offset facility is available only on computerised numerically controlled machines. Once the offset has been established the slide movement is automatically adjusted as required during the program run.

An offset can therefore be defined as a dimensional value defining the position of the cutting edge, or edges, of a tool in relation to a given datum.

Tool length offsets

Consider the component shown in Figure 3.20(a). The programmer has decided that the Z datum clearance plane will be 2 mm above the top face of the work. All tool movement in the Z axis will be in relation to that datum. The machine setter or operator will establish the datum either by 'touching on' to the work surface and moving away 2 mm or by touching on to a suitable 2 mm thick setting block, and then setting the Z axis readout to zero.

Now consider the tooling shown in Figure 3.20(b) and assume the tool T01 has been set as described above. This is now the master tool. However, the machining that is required also involves using tools T02 and T03 and the position of their cutting edges in the Z axis does not correspond to that of tool T01. Tool T02 is too short and tool T03 is too long. Any movements in relation to the Z zero axis involving these tools must take into account their starting position.

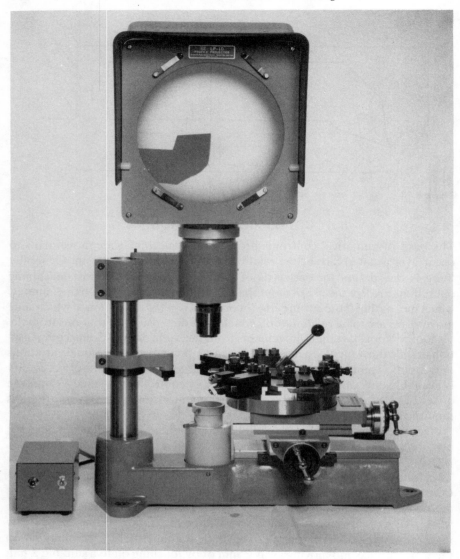

Figure 3.19 *Pre-setting tooling on a replacement turret using optical projection.*

The tool setter or machine operator must therefore establish the length and direction of movement which is necessary to bring the end of each tool to the zero position. This can be done by touching each tool on to the setting block and noting on the digital readout its variation from zero. Tool T02 will require a movement in the *Z* axis of 5.38 mm and tool T03 a movement of −4.91 mm. These dimensions are the tool length offsets.

Having established the offsets, the operator records them either by setting a

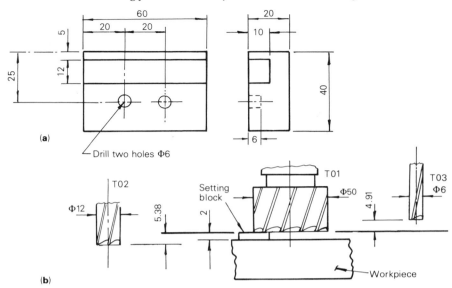

Figure 3.20 **(a)** *Component detail* **(b)** *tool length offsets for the milling/drilling operation.*

series of numbered thumb-wheel switches or, as is the case with most modern control units, by entering them via the control panel into an offset file or page which can be displayed on the controller visual display screen. The method of entering offsets and the display format vary according to the control unit. The entry for the offsets relating to the tooling in Figure 3.20 could appear as shown in Figure 3.21.

With the tool length offsets being established at the machine, the part programmer is now able to ignore the variations in tool length and write the program on the assumption that all tools are starting their movements from the Z axis zero datum.

Tool length offsets are not confined to milling. They are also applicable to turning, but in this case two offset lengths are involved, one in the X axis and the other in the Z axis. The set of tools with varying lengths shown in Figure 3.22 illustrates the situation, while Figure 3.23 shows how the necessary offsets would be entered in an offset file.

Tool radius offsets

Just as cutting tools vary in length, they may also vary in diameter or, in the case of turning tools, in the radius of the tool tip.

Consider the profile shown in Figure 3.24. This profile could be machined by a cutter of, say, 15 mm diameter or 30 mm diameter and the path of each cutter will vary as indicated. Similarly, the profile of the component shown in Figure 3.25 could be turned using a tool with a tip radius of 1 or 2 mm and again the cutter paths will vary.

TOOL OFFSET FILE

T	LENGTH	DIAMETER
1	0.0000	50.0000
2	5.3800	12.0000
3	−4.9100	6.0000
4	0.0000	0.0000
5	0.0000	0.0000
6	0.0000	0.0000
7	0.0000	0.0000
8	0.0000	0.0000
9	0.0000	0.0000
10	0.0000	0.0000
11	0.0000	0.0000
12	0.0000	0.0000
13	0.0000	0.0000
14	0.0000	0.0000

METRIC (applies to column at left)

Figure 3.21 *Tool offset file for milling.*

Without a cutter radius compensation facility the programmer would have to state the precise size of the cutting tools to be used and program the machine slide movements accordingly. With the facility the cutter size can be ignored and the work profile programmed. The exact size of the cutting tool to be used for machining is entered by the operator into the offset file and when the offset is called into the program automatic compensation in slide movement will be made.

For milling machines the cutter size is entered as a diameter, as shown in Figure 3.21, and the machine slide movement is compensated by half of the dimensional entry. For turning centres the offset will be entered as a radius alongside the tool length offsets, as shown in Figure 3.23.

Cutter radius compensation can be to the right or left of a profile. To determine which is applicable the programmer should imagine a position above the tool facing the direction in which cutting is taking place. Thus cutter radius compensation to machine the profile shown in Figure 3.24 would be to the left.

Tool offsets can be entered, modified or erased by the machine operator at will and so it is possible to use the facility to:

(a) accommodate replacement tooling which varies dimensionally from the original;
(b) make variations to the component size;

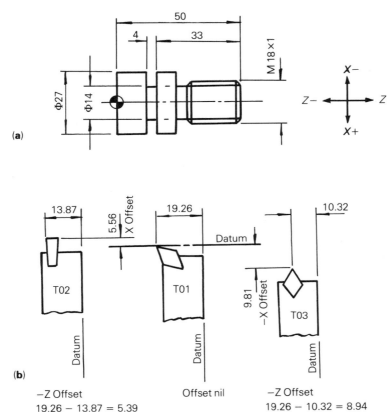

Figure 3.22 **(a)** *Component detail* **(b)** *tool length offsets for a turning operation.*

(c) initiate a series of cuts, say roughing and finishing, using the same dimensional program data.

While offsets have a direct effect on the machining currently being carried out, they do not affect the basic part program.

Identification of cutter offsets

Reference again to Figures 3.21 and 3.23 will show that the offsets are numbered. In a similar way tooling used in any part program is given a numerical identity. The two, tools and offsets, have to be related to each other when the part program is being made. The number of tool stations on any one machine is limited, perhaps 12 to 16 on a turning centre to rather more on machining centres equipped with magazines. The number of offsets available will be greater than the number of tools available so that any tool can be used with any offset. Thus if the tools are numbered T01, T02, T03, T04 and so on,

TOOL OFFSET FILE	T	X	Z	RADIUS
	1	0.0000	0.0000	2.0000
	2	5.5600	−5.3900	0.0000
METRIC	3	−9.8100	−8.9400	1.5000
	4	0.0000	0.0000	0.0000
	5	0.0000	0.0000	0.0000
	6	0.0000	0.0000	0.0000
	7	0.0000	0.0000	0.0000
	8	0.0000	0.0000	0.0000
	9	0.0000	0.0000	0.0000
	10	0.0000	0.0000	0.0000
	11	0.0000	0.0000	0.0000
	12	0.0000	0.0000	0.0000
	13	0.0000	0.0000	0.0000
	14	0.0000	0.0000	0.0000

Figure 3.23   *Tool offset file for turning.*

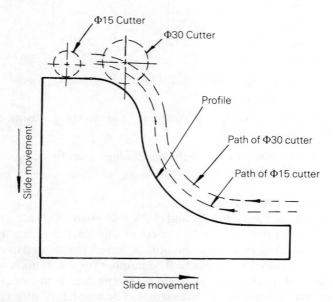

Figure 3.24   *Cutter radius offset for milling operation.*

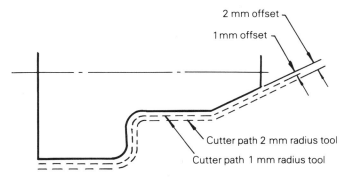

Figure 3.25 *Cutter radius offset for turning operation.*

and the offsets are numbered 01 to 32, the programmer may call for tool number one to be used with offset number one. The data entry in the part program would read T0101. It follows that, since there are more offsets available than tools, the program could well call for the same tool to be used elsewhere with yet another offset, say T0106. It is imperative that the programmer's intentions are clearly relayed to the shop floor. (See 'Documentation associated with part programming', Chapter 8.)

TOOL CONTROL

The efficient use of expensive numerically controlled machining facilities requires a very methodical approach to the provision of tooling. It is essential that the tooling, both original and replacement, available at the machine correspond to the tooling required by the part program. Close co-operation between personnel concerned with programming, tool preparation and machining must be maintained.

Efficient tool control should provide for the following functions:

(a) reconditioning, including re-grinding when appropriate, replacing damaged or worn inserts, etc.;
(b) preparation, including sizing, pre-setting, identifying, etc.;
(c) storage in a tool library;
(d) transportation;
(e) storage alongside the machine.

The concept is illustrated diagrammatically in Figure 3.26.

Tools that can be reconditioned by grinding require skilled attention. Cutting efficiency over long periods of machining at very high rates of metal removal

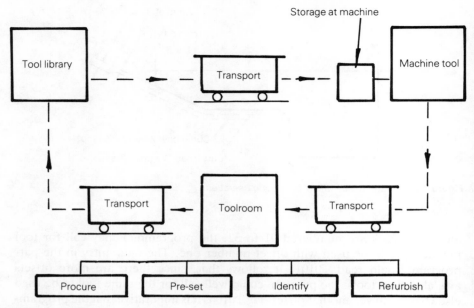

Figure 3.26 *Tool control system.*

demands exact tool geometry. The less than precise methods often applied to tooling used on conventional machines are not acceptable for numerically controlled machining.

The accuracy demanded and the nature of the equipment used when pre-setting or establishing the precise size of tools call for skilled personnel working in clean conditions.

As tooling is prepared it must immediately be marked to facilitate identification. This can be done in a number of ways, but one method which is widely used is to place the tool in an adjustable holder to which is attached a magnetised vinyl marker card. Identification will of course correspond to the tool identity allocated by the part programmer and the tool preparation will be based on instructions he or she has prepared.

The storage of tooling not immediately required in a tool library requires the use of heavy-duty steel racks in which the tools, in their identity holders when used, can be accommodated.

Transport of sets of tooling about the plant will require suitable trolleys. In some cases, to reduce handling, such trolleys are used for storage at the machine. If space on the shop floor is restricted, transfer to a stand may be more appropriate. One example of such a stand is referred to as a 'tool wheel', since it rotates to facilitate access to each tool; this is shown in Figure 3.27.

Figure 3.27 *Tool storage wheel.*

QUESTIONS

1   When are high-speed steel-cutting tools likely to be used in CNC machining?

2   When are solid carbide tools, as opposed to tips, likely to be used in CNC machining?

3   Why are solid carbide tools not widely used?

4   State three advantages of using indexable inserts.

5   State two methods used to control swarf when using indexable inserts.

6   What is the significance of the letters P, M and K in relation to the classification of carbide grades?

7   How are carbide inserts classified?

8   What is the difference between a holder and a cartridge?

9   Make an outline sketch of a tool suitable for use on a turning centre and explain the meaning of the term 'qualified'.

10   How many methods of locating and clamping inserts in holders and cartridges are included in the ISO code?

11   The following is the specification for a tool holder: M P D F L 40 40 D 24 F. What is the meaning of each letter or number?

12   Explain the difference between a tool turret and a tool magazine.

13   If a machining program is to remain valid when tool replacement is carried out, one of two conditions must be met. What are those conditions?

14   Explain with the aid of a simple diagram what is meant by pre-set tooling.

15   What is a tool length offset and when is it likely to be necessary?

16   What is cutter radius compensation and how does it simplify programming?

17   How is it possible to determine whether cutter compensation is to the right or left of a machined profile?

18   List the functions of an efficient tool control system.

19   What is the function of a tool library?

20   What is a tool wheel and when it is used?

4

WORK HOLDING AND LOADING FOR NUMERICALLY CONTROLLED MACHINING

THE APPLICATION OF COMMON WORK-HOLDING DEVICES

The basic requirements of any work-holding device are that it must:

(a) securely hold the work;
(b) provide positive location;
(c) be quick and easy to operate.

There are a variety of devices in general use that have been tried and tested in conventional machining situations. Chucks, collets and vices are obvious examples, and these are also used on numerically controlled machines. Work-holding devices such as these may be mechanical, pneumatic or hydraulic in operation. Mechanically operated devices usually involve manual intervention and, although it is not uncommon to see workpieces being loaded and clamped in this way, it is not a practice which is in keeping with automatic machining processes. Because of this, hydraulic or pneumatically operated devices, especially the latter, are favoured. The operation of hydraulic or pneumatic clamping is easily controlled electronically via the machine control unit and also provides for rapid operation and uniform clamping pressure. The application of a power-operated collet is shown in Figure 4.1 and a power-operated chuck is shown in Figure 4.2.

Conventional devices such as these are more suited to machining where the component or the stock material is uniform in shape, that is, rectangular, round, hexagonal, etc. Components of irregular shape, such as castings, can be accommodated, as with conventional machining, on purpose-built fixtures sometimes incorporating pneumatic or hydraulic clamping arrangements.

THE IMPORTANCE OF ACCURATE LOCATION

It is established working practice that, wherever possible, work should be positively located, that is, it should be positioned in such a way that when the cutting forces are applied there can be no possibility of movement taking place.

Figure 4.1 *Use of collet for work holding on a turning centre.*

Figure 4.3 shows two applications of a conventional machine vice. In both cases the work is located against the fixed jaw but in Figure 4.3(a) the security of the workpiece depends on a frictional hold and the cutting force could result in movement of the workpiece. In Figure 4.3(b) no movement is possible since the fixed jaw of the vice not only locates the workpiece but also absorbs the forces resulting from the cutting action.

Figure 4.2 *Use of power-operated chuck on a turning centre.*

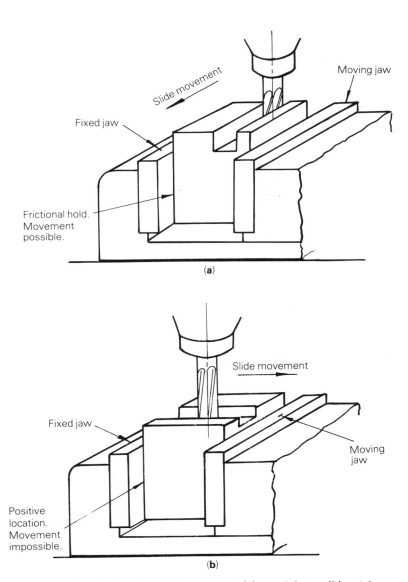

Figure 4.3 *Positive location of a milled component* **(a)** *unsatisfactory* **(b)** *satisfactory.*

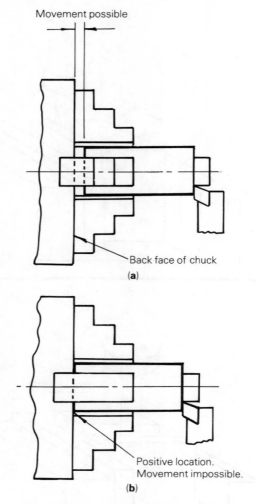

Figure 4.4 *Positive location of a turned component* **(a)** *unsatisfactory* **(b)** *satisfactory.*

Similarly, in Figure 4.4(a) it can be seen that it is possible for the workpiece held in the chuck to move, since it is not positively located. Figure 4.4(b) shows how the possibility of movement is eliminated by using the back face of the chuck for positive location.

In any machining process the possibility of movement of the workpiece is unacceptable for safety reasons. In numerically controlled machining processes there is also the problem that movement, however slight, means a loss of dimensional accuracy since there is generally no constant monitoring of the workpiece size as machining proceeds. Additionally, the location of the component is often directly related to the part program, since the programmer, when writing the program, will establish datums on which all numerical data controlling the machine slide movements will be based. If the component is not precisely positioned in relation to those datums then the machining features required will not be achieved.

Figure 4.5(a) shows a component which is to be machined on a vertical machining centre, and the datum in the X and Y axes which the programmer has established as a basis for the part program.

The machine setter will be informed of the position of the datum, either by written instructions or possibly via messages included as part of the program and visually displayed on the machine control unit, and he or she will be required to set the work-holding device, which in turn provides the precise location for the component, accordingly.

To illustrate the need for accurate component location consider again Figure 4.5. Clearly a workpiece positioned as shown in (b) will not have the same dimensional features in the X axis as the component position shown in (c). In this particular case the logical thing to do would be to place all components as shown in (d), thus using the end of the vice jaw as a locating position, and set the machine datum accordingly. A plate attached to the side of the fixed jaw is a method which can be used to ensure perfect location.

Figure 4.6 shows the use of a self-centring chuck where the back face provides the datum and location face in the Z axis and the self-centring action provides the datum and location in the X axis. The positioning of the workpiece to establish positive location in the X axis is automatic, but the machine setter will need to be informed that the work is to be located against the back face of the chuck to maintain the dimensional validity of the part program in the Z axis.

When the bar size is smaller than the machine spindle bore, accurate location may still be achieved by using a setting plate placed against the back face of the chuck and against which the component is located prior to clamping. The plate is removed before machining commences and so the positive location, that is, a location where the possibility of movement is completely removed, does not exist. An alternative to using a setting plate is to use soft jaws bored to suit.

THE USE OF GRID PLATES FOR MILLING AND DRILLING

A method of work holding and location that has gained wide acceptance for numerically controlled milling and drilling set-ups is the grid plate.

A grid plate is simply a base plate made of steel or cast iron which is drilled with a series of accurately positioned holes. These holes may be tapped to facilitate clamping, plain reamed to accommodate location dowels, or tapped and counter-bored to provide for clamping and location. Each hole can be identified using the grid system illustrated in Figure 4.7.

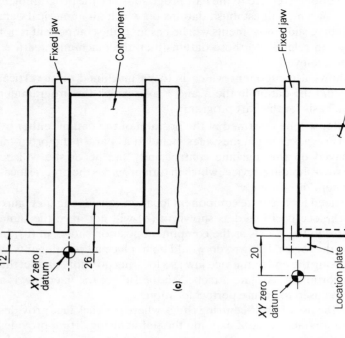

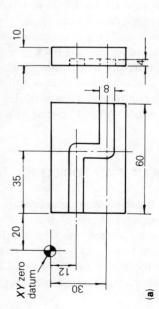

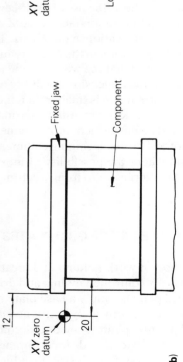

Figure 4.5 *Relationship between setting position and part program for a milled component* **(a)** *component detail* **(b)** *initial setting* **(c)** *second setting* **(d)** *setting position constant, no variation in component size.*

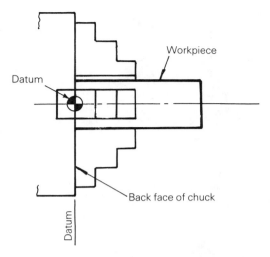

Figure 4.6 *Accurate location of a turned component providing constant datum position.*

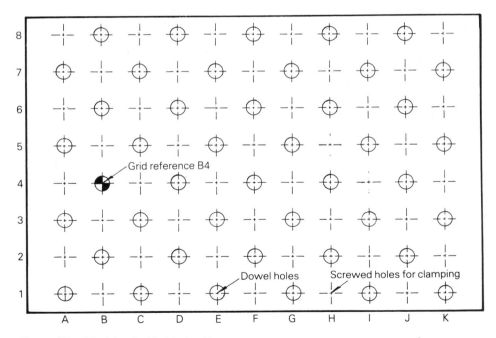

Figure 4.7 *Principle of grid plate location.*

Figure 4.8   *Grid plate showing three components in position.*

The grid plate is attached to the machine table, often permanently, and since the part programmer can identify the exact position of any holes and will know the dimensions of any locating dowels or blocks used in the work-holding arrangement, he or she can establish datums when writing the program and instruct the machine setter accordingly.

The setting of a grid plate does not involve the use of dial indicators, feeler gauges, etc. and therefore is not demanding on manual skills on the shop floor. Once set it provides for quick, simple and accurate location of the workpiece.

It is often possible to load more than one component at each setting and at known pitches. By using the 'zero shift' facility (see Chapter 6) the machining program can be repeated in a new position with a resulting saving in machine down time.

Apart from clamping directly to the grid plate, components can be held in vices, or a set of vices, which themselves are accurately located and clamped in position. Complex shapes can be accommodated by using specially shaped locators while fixtures can be provided with locating devices so that they may be accurately located and clamped in a known position.

Through cutting is possible by using stepped locators which raise the work-piece from the grid plate.

Figure 4.9 *Vertical application of a grid plate.*

Examples of commercially available grid plates for both horizontal and vertical applications are shown in Figures 4.8 and 4.9.

THE USE OF ROTARY TABLES AND INDEXERS
FOR MILLING AND DRILLING

Many of the conventional uses of a rotary table have become redundant with the introduction of numerical control. Radial profiles are now achieved by circular interpolation, and the positioning of holes or slots in angular relationship to each other, using polar co-ordinates, has been reduced to nothing more complex than a simple data entry in the machine program. Circular interpolation and polar co-ordinates are discussed in more detail in Chapter 6.

Rotary tables are still used on horizontal machines for rotating work to facilitate machining in a new position in the vertical plane. An angle of rotation of 90°, for example, permits machining on four sides of a cube, but the facility can be used to rotate the work through much smaller angles. An angle of rotation as small as 1° is common.

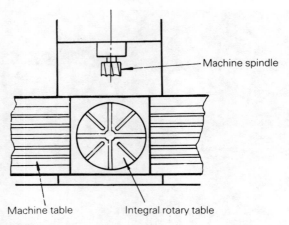

Figure 4.10 *Integral rotary table.*

Rotary tables of this type may be attached to the machine bed in the normal way or be a built-in feature of the machine table, as illustrated in Figure 4.10.

Conventional dividing heads are also redundant as far as numerical control is concerned. They have been replaced by hydraulic indexers, fully programmable and controlled via the machining program. Simple versions cater for up to 24 positions, or increments of 15°, rather like the direct indexing plate fitted to conventional dividing heads.

For more complex indexing or where continual rotation is required, for example when cutting a helix, a rather more sophisticated version is needed. Some of these devices are capable of rotating in two planes. (Rather confusingly they are referred to as 'tilting rotary tables' by one manufacturer.) When the two-axis version is used in conjunction with three axes of table movement, thus providing a five-axis machining capability, it permits the production of components so complex that they may well be incapable of being produced by conventional means.

THE USE OF PALLETS FOR MILLING AND DRILLING

An aim of production engineers is to minimise down time, that is, time when the machine is not fulfilling its prime function of cutting metal. A major source of down time is work loading and unloading. The use of pre-loaded pallets considerably improves the situation.

A pallet is simply a table which, like the grid plate, is provided with a series of holes or slots to facilitate location and clamping of the component. Pallets are fitted to the machines shown in Figures 2.1(b) and 3.14.

The most simple arrangement will involve the use of just two pallets. A work-

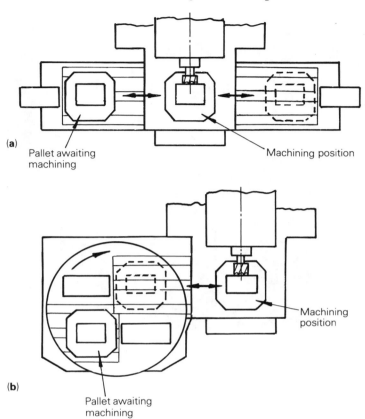

(a) Pallet awaiting machining

Machining position

(b) Pallet awaiting machining

Machining position

Figure 4.11 *Pallet shuttles* **(a)** *linear* **(b)** *rotary.*

piece is located and clamped on the first pallet in a position predetermined by the part programmer and the pallet is then moved into the machining position. As machining is taking place the second pallet is loaded. When machining of the first component is complete the pallets are interchanged and as the second component is being machined the first pallet is unloaded and re-loaded with another component.

Pallets can be interchanged in several ways. Two such methods, one involving a shuttle system and the other a rotary movement, are illustrated in Figure 4.11(a) and (b). Some machining systems involve more than two pallets (see Chapter 9).

WORK SUPPORT FOR TURNING OPERATIONS

The majority of turned components are relatively small. The work-holding arrangements employed in their production are conventional, that is, chucks

Figure 4.12   *Use of a tailstock for work support on a turning centre.*

and collets are used and there is no need for further work support. Because of this a number of the smaller turning centres available do not have tailstocks. They are no longer essential for drilling, reaming, etc., as this work is carried out from the turret.

When the capacity of the machine is such that the work overhang can be considerable, then tailstock support becomes essential. It is also necessary, of course, for turning between centres. Figure 4.12 illustrates a tailstock being used on a numerically controlled turning centre.

On some machines the tailstock is very similar to that of a conventional centre lathe. It is positioned and clamped solely by manual intervention. On others it is semi-controlled, being manually positioned and clamped on the machine bed but with a programmable hydraulic quill movement. Some machines provide for a fully programmable tailstock, that is, both its position along the bed and the quill movement, together with the necessary clamping, can be included in the part program and automatically controlled.

If a fully programmed tailstock movement is to be used it is essential that, as the quill moves forward, the workpiece is in the correct position, that is, on centre in order to receive the centre support. Acknowledging that this condition may be difficult to obtain, some manufacturers offer hydraulic self-centring steadies to position the work prior to the tailstock movement being made.

Figure 4.13   *Bar steady providing pressure-controlled support.*

Steadies are also available to prevent the deflection of slender work, these being located on the machine bed in a manner similar to the way steadies are employed on conventional lathes. Two types of steadies are illustrated in Figures 4.13 and 4.14.

WORK LOADING FOR TURNING OPERATIONS

Work loading into turning centres may be manual or automatic. The choice of method to be used will be affected by various factors such as component size, component shape and quantity required.

Manual loading detracts from the benefits in terms of increased production rates and reduced labour costs inherent in numerically controlled machining. However, it is quite acceptable for small-batch production and indeed may be essential when the component shape is irregular, for example, a casting, or when non-standard work-holding devices, such as a fixture clamped to a face plate, are being used.

When automatic loading is applicable the cost of the necessary equipment is likely to be the determining factor in the final choice. The possibilities range from relatively inexpensive bar feeders to arrangements involving conveyors and robots.

Figure 4.14   *Mechanically adjusted bar steady.*

Bar feeders have been applied to turning machines for many years. One of the disadvantages associated with earlier designs was that they were noisy in operation, the noise being created by the bar rotating in the feeder tube. Modern designs have eliminated this problem by various methods, perhaps the most successful one being where the bar is completely surrounded by oil. The bar is fed into the machine under pressure (hydraulic and pneumatic systems are available) when the work-holding device releases its grip. The bar extends to a pre-set stop located in the turret before the work-holding device closes again.

Bar feeders do not provide total automation, since they have to be reloaded manually from time to time. A modern bar feeder is shown in Figure 4.15.

Components that are too large for bar feeders to be suitable are often produced from pre-prepared 'billets', that is, the material is supplied in short lengths, sometimes already faced to size. Material in this form, and part machined components of similar size requiring further machining, are usually

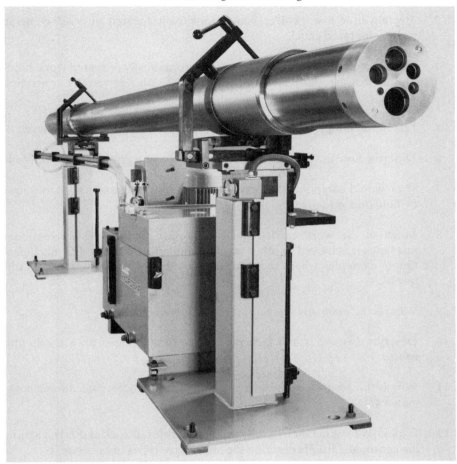

Figure 4.15 *Silent bar feeder. Bar is supported in oil.*

suitable for robot handling. Many machine manufacturers offer robot handling equipment as an optional extra, the robot being adaptable to various component shapes and sizes by fitting interchangeable end effectors (grippers).

QUESTIONS

1   Explain what is meant by positive location as applied to work holding.

2   Why is it especially important that components are positively located for numerically controlled machining operations?

3   Explain how a workpiece can be positively located in a self-centring power-operated chuck.

4   State three reasons why pneumatic or hydraulically operated work-holding devices are particularly suitable for use on numerically controlled machines.

5   List the advantages of the grid plate as a means of holding workpieces.

6   Describe how the positioning of a workpiece on a grid plate is identified.

7   How would components of irregular shape, such as castings or forgings, be held on a grid plate?

8   Much of the work carried out on a rotary table using conventional machines is achieved in other ways on numerically controlled machines. Quote examples where the facilities provided by a rotary table are still useful.

9   What is the main advantage of using pre-loaded pallets?

10   Describe two ways in which pallets are interchanged on a machining centre.

11   Why is the accurate location of a pallet essential before machining commences?

12   Explain what is meant by a fully programmable tailstock as used on a turning centre and briefly describe the alternative types of tailstock.

13   What is the main disadvantage of having manual work loading in a numerically controlled machining situation? Give an example of a situation where there is unlikely to be an economically viable alternative.

14   What are the advantages and disadvantages of using bar feeders for turning centres?

15   What are billets and what are the advantages in their use?

5

DATA PREPARATION AND INPUT TO MACHINE CONTROL UNITS

DATA PREPARATION

The preparation of numerical data prior to input to the machine control unit is referred to as programming. The extent of the preparation will depend on the complexity of the component. It is possible that the data necessary to produce a simple component may require nothing more than an examination of a detailed drawing followed by a direct manual entry to the control unit. On the other hand, programming very complex components may require computing facilities to determine appropriate tool paths. The vast majority of components require an approach similar to that outlined diagrammatically in Figure 5.1.

From the diagram it can be seen that the program is central to the whole process. It is compiled after taking into account a number of essential inter-related factors and then, having been compiled, it totally controls the machining process. Efficient programming requires considerable practical knowledge on the part of the programmer together with a full understanding of the control system to be employed.

The approach to programming must be methodical, and because of this it usually involves compiling a special form or listing the data on a computer screen, preferably followed by a checking process, before recording the data in a form acceptable to the machine control unit. Even at this late stage a further checking process, referred to as 'program proving', is essential before a final commitment to machining is made.

DATA INPUT

Data can be entered into machine control units by the following methods:

1. Manual data input (MDI).
2. Conversational manual data input.
3. Perforated tape.
4. Magnetic tape.
5. Magnetic disc.
6. Master computer (direct numerical control, DNC).

85

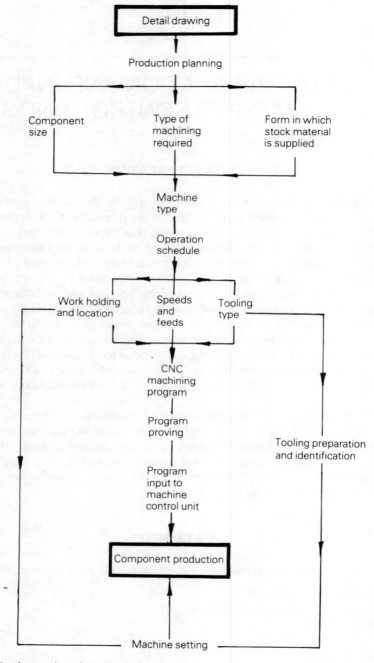

Figure 5.1 *Approach to data preparation.*

Manual data input

Manual data input is used when setting the machine and editing programs, and for entering complete programs, although the latter should be restricted to relatively simple programs so that the machine is not idle for too long as the data entry is being made.

Manual data input to NC machines To input data on non-computerised control units the operator has to set dials, position switches, etc. before finally activating the machine tool to carry out the required movements. Only a limited amount of data can be entered at any one time. Data-recording facilities are often not available.

Manual data input to CNC machines On computerised control units, by pressing the appropriate buttons on the control console a limited amount of data or a complete part program may be entered and the machine activated accordingly. The computer will retain the data and it can be transferred to a recording medium such as magnetic tape or disc and transferred back to the computer as and when required.

Conversational manual data input

Conversational manual data input involves the operator pressing the appropriate keys on the control console in response to questions in everyday English which appear on the visual display unit (VDU) screen. This method of manual data input is quicker than methods which require the use of data codes, and manufacturers of these control units claim that to make the first chip takes one tenth of the time and operator training is just a matter of hours as opposed to up to two weeks for non-conversational input.

The basis of conversational data input is the pre-programming of the computer with standard data stored in files within the computer memory, each item of data being numerically identified and called into the program by the appropriate operator response.

Consider the turning of a bar of metal on a turning centre. Before any consideration can be given to slide movements, the basic metal-cutting data would have to be ascertained. For example, the correct spindle speed and feed rate are of vital importance. The spindle speed is affected by the work diameter and the cutting speed. The cutting speed is related to the material being machined. The feed rate would depend on the depth of cut, tool type and surface finish required. From this it can be seen that the necessary data to machine the metal successfully can be related to four factors:

(a) the material being cut;
(b) the material diameter;
(c) the surface finish required;
(d) the tool type.

MATERIAL STOCK FILE	
CODE	MATERIAL
1	MILD STEEL
2	MED. CARBON STEEL
3	STAINLESS STEEL
4	CAST IRON
5	DURALUMIN

SURFACE ROUGHNESS FILE	
CODE	Ra
1	100
2	50
3	25
4	12.5
5	6.3

Figure 5.2 *Material file and surface roughness file.*

The computer will be programmed to select the appropriate spindle speed and feed rate from an input of information relating to these factors. To assist the input of information there will be a material file and surface roughness file within the computer memory, as shown in Figure 5.2.

Cutting tools available will also be numerically identified. A simple question-and-answer routine will extract from the computer memory all the necessary data to give the correct cutting conditions, the programmer being relieved of making any calculations or judgements whatsoever. An example of a question-and-answer routine is as follows:

VDU question	*Operator's keyed response*
Material?	5 input
Material diameter?	50 input
Surface code?	4 input
Tool number?	8 input

The above illustrates just a small part of the total data input necessary to make a component, and having established basic cutting conditions the programmer would proceed to feed in further data relating to slide movement, etc. However, even slide movement data input can be reduced to a question-and-answer routine, even when the movements are complex, such as when machining a radius or cutting a screw thread.

Consider the production of a thread on a work diameter that has just been produced by the preceding data entry. The required data input may be restricted to the following questions:

> Thread root diameter?
> Pitch?
> Number of starts?

From this the control will determine the number of passes necessary, the depth of cut taken by each pass and the feed rate needed to produce the required pitch. Even the spindle speed may vary automatically to cater for roughing and finishing cuts.

Routines such as the one described are commonly known as 'canned cycles' and are not restricted to conversational MDI but may also form part of other programming systems. The use of such routines is described in more detail in Chapter 6.

Data entered in response to questions can be recorded, usually on magnetic tape, for future use. Some advanced conversational MDI systems incorporate the use of computer graphics (see 'Graphical numerical control', Chapter 9).

Perforated tape input

Not so long ago numerical control was generally referred to as tape control, an indication of the important part this input medium has played in the development of the technology. The expression is not quite so common as it was, but perforated tape is still widely used.

The basis of tape control is the transfer of coded information contained on a perforated tape to the machine control unit via a tape reader.

The standard tape width is 25 mm. Originally only paper tape was used, and it is still the most popular material, a factor very much in its favour being its low cost. It is available in rolls or precisely folded in a concertina or fan-like arrangement. The rolls are most commonly used, but the folded paper is possibly easier to store.

One of the problems with paper tape is that the sprocket drive holes which are used to carry the tape through some tape readers tend to wear or even tear. Also, a tape can easily be damaged by contact with oil, which is always likely in a workshop. This has led to the introduction of other materials or combinations of materials, but while these tapes are more durable they are usually more expensive.

Examples of tape materials other than paper include polyester film, paper–polyester–paper laminates, polyester–aluminium-foil–polyester laminates and metallised polyester. Some of these tapes can cause excessive punch wear and the adhesives used to produce some laminates have also presented punching problems.

The choice of tape is also affected by the tape reader being used. The prime function of the reader is to detect the presence and position of the perforations in the tape. Tape readers may be mechanical, pneumatic or photo-electrical. A photo-electric tape reader is illustrated in Figure 5.3.

Mechanical tape readers use 'fingers' to detect the perforations. Pneumatic readers involve air under pressure passing through the perforations. Photo-electric readers have light either passing through the perforations or being reflected from a reflector positioned behind the tape. Having detected a perforation the reader converts this information into an electrical signal which is transmitted to the control unit.

Pneumatic tape readers are not very common, but they generally employ plain paper tape. Mechanical readers require a strong tape due to the physical contact between the tape and the locating fingers, so a paper–polythene–paper laminated tape is likely to be recommended. Electrical readers using the reflective principle will require a tape with a non-reflective surface finish or colour, while the direct light readers require tapes that are not translucent.

The qualities required of tapes used in photo-electric tape readers have resulted in a variety of colours being used. Some tapes are dual coloured, which helps to reduce the possibility of reverse loading in the readers.

Figure 5.3 *Photo-electric tape reader.*

Reverse loading is also prevented by the offset of the sprocket holes when used, while feed direction is indicated by arrows printed on the tape. In addition to this, when the tape is severed from the main roll after punching, the leading end will be pointed and the trailing end will have a corresponding recess.

The advent of the computer as an integral part of control systems has minimised the strength and wear problems associated with plain paper tapes. On older control units the tape is run through the reader each time a component is machined. For short programs it can be spliced to form a continuous loop, thus eliminating the need for rewinding. For longer programs the tape is wound from reel to reel. Now it is common practice to use the tape more as a storage medium, feeding the data it contains into the control unit computer by just one pass through the tape reader. The computer retains the data in its memory and this facilitates data retrieval as and when required. When data are transferred from tape to the computer memory the tape can be removed from the reader to avoid contamination.

Tape standards and the binary code   When a tape reader detects a perforation the transmission of an electrical signal to the control unit results. The simplest way an electrical signal can be meaningful is by its presence or absence, creating an on–off effect. The detection of a perforation registers an 'on' signal, and this signal will be given further meaning by the position of the perforation which caused it, as will be explained later.

Whatever the type of tape reader, the switching effect is achieved by using binary arithmetic, a system which has two as a base and can convey numerical values in terms of 1 and 0: 'on' and 'off'.

To understand the binary system of numbers it is helpful to look more closely at the familiar decimal or denary system, which uses ten as a base. In this system numerical values are constructed from multiples of units, tens, hundreds, thousands, etc.

$$
\begin{aligned}
\text{Unit} && 1 &= 10^0 \\
\text{Ten} && 10 &= 10^1 \\
\text{Hundred} && 100 &= 10^2 \\
\text{Thousand} && 1000 &= 10^3
\end{aligned}
$$

Thus the number 2345 is made up as follows:

Thousand (10^3)	Hundred (10^2)	Ten (10^1)	Unit (10^0)
2	3	4	5

This is a convenient, well understood method of expressing numbers, but unfortunately it does not readily relate to the requirements of electrical switching control.

Now consider the application of the binary system using two as the base—2^0, 2^1, 2^2, 2^3, and so on—and then relate this to certain denary values as follows:

$$
\begin{aligned}
\text{Let} \quad 2^0 &= 1 \\
\text{Then} \quad 2^1 &= 2 \\
2^2 &= 4 \\
2^3 &= 8 \text{ and so on}
\end{aligned}
$$

By using this small range of binary values any decimal digit can be expressed as shown in Table 5.1.

Table 5.1 Decimal digits expressed in binary.

Decimal digit	Binary equivalent				Composition
	2^3	2^2	2^1	2^0	
1				1	$2^0 = 1$
2			1	0	$2^1 + 0 = 2$
3			1	1	$2^1 + 2^0 = 3$
4		1	0	0	$2^2 + 0 + 0 = 4$
5		1	0	1	$2^2 + 0 + 2^0 = 5$
6		1	1	0	$2^2 + 2^1 + 0 = 6$
7		1	1	1	$2^2 + 2^1 + 2^0 = 7$
8	1	0	0	0	$2^3 + 0 + 0 + 0 = 8$
9	1	0	0	1	$2^3 + 0 + 0 + 2^0 = 9$

Now if the holes in the perforated control tape are arranged in columns or tracks corresponding to the binary values indicated in Table 5.1 it is possible to express the required denary values by making perforations in the appropriate places. The number 2345, for example, would be indicated as follows:

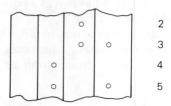

2
3
4
5

The tape shown above has, for the purpose of simplifying the explanation, only four tracks or vertical rows of holes. This is all that is required to express numbers. However, the numbers used in numerical control need an identity; for example, a slide movement not only has a dimensional value but the axis in which movement is required has to be defined. This definition is achieved by using letters, as explained in Chapter 1.

There are two tape standards in general use, the ISO (International Standards Organisation) and the EIA (Electrical Industries Association); the latter was developed in the United States of America and gained wide acceptance before the introduction of the ISO standards. The two tapes identify letters in different ways, and the following description is applicable only to the ISO standard.

The 26 letters of the alphabet are identified numerically from 1 to 26. We have seen that the digits 1 to 9 can be expressed using four binary columns. To include the numbers 10 to 26 requires a fifth column, a fifth track in the tape, so that the decimal value can be expressed *in one row* of punched holes, as shown in Table 5.2.

Table 5.2   Letters of the alphabet expressed numerically.

Letter	Decimal digit	2^4	2^3	2^2	2^1	2^0	Composition
			Binary equivalent				
J	10		1	0	1	0	$2^3 + 0 + 2^1 + 0 = 10$
K	11		1	0	1	1	$2^3 + 0 + 2^1 + 2^0 = 11$
L	12		1	1	0	0	$2^3 + 2^2 + 0 + 0 = 12$
M	13		1	1	0	1	$2^3 + 2^2 + 0 + 2^0 = 13$
N	14		1	1	1	0	$2^3 + 2^2 + 2^1 + 0 = 14$
O	15		1	1	1	1	$2^3 + 2^2 + 2^1 + 2^0 = 15$
P	16	1	0	0	0	0	$2^4 + 0 + 0 + 0 + 0 = 16$
Q	17	1	0	0	0	1	$2^4 + 0 + 0 + 0 + 2^0 = 17$
R	18	1	0	0	1	0	$2^4 + 0 + 0 + 2^1 + 0 = 18$
S	19	1	0	0	1	1	$2^4 + 0 + 0 + 2^1 + 2^0 = 19$

There is, of course, a conflict as far as the first nine decimal digits are concerned. Does the value indicated, 7 for example, indicate a numerical value or the seventh letter, G? This is clarified by increasing the number of tracks in the tape from five to seven. Digits are indicated by additional holes being punched in both tracks five and six, while letters are indicated by holes punched in track 7.

The control system will require other characters as well as numbers and letters. For instance, a minus (−) sign may be necessary to indicate the direction of slide movement. These additional symbols have been allocated combinations of punched holes not used otherwise.

Finally, to check the accuracy of the tape punching and tape reading, there is an eighth track referred to as a parity track. The ISO standard requires that each row contain an even number of holes. If the required character is expressed by an odd number of holes an extra hole will be punched in track eight. If the required character is expressed by an even number of holes there will be no extra hole in track eight. This sytem is referred to as 'even parity'. The EIA system also uses an eighth track, but has 'odd parity'. A visual check that each line of the tape contains an even number of holes (ISO) or an odd number of holes (EIA) is one method of ascertaining that there are no errors as a result of the equipment malfunctioning. Both tapes are referred to as 'eight bit'. 'Eight' refers to the number of tracks and 'bit' is derived from <u>BI</u>nary digi<u>T</u>.

By reference to Figure 5.4 the reader can see the variations between the two tape standards. Most modern control systems will accept either standard.

Tape format Each horizontal row of holes in the tape is termed a 'character'. Each set of characters is termed a 'word'. Each set of words is termed a 'block'. This is illustrated in Figure 5.5.

Blocks are identified by the letter N followed by three digits. A block will contain information on the type of slide movement required, length of slide movement, rate of slide movement, spindle speed, tool identity, etc. and terminate with an 'end of block' character.

The order in which words are entered in a block may be fixed or variable. The fixed block format requires each block to have the correct number of entries and they must appear in a set sequence. This means that data have to be re-entered in each block even if there has been no change from the previous block and even if the numerical value of the entry is zero. On some systems each word has to be separated by the *tab* function, this type of format being referred to as *tab sequential*.

Much more commonly used is the variable block format in which words can be entered in any order. Their meaning or function is determined by the letter preceding the data, a system referred to as *word address*. Data which remain unchanged in following blocks need not be re-entered, and this leads to more rapid programming and a considerable reduction in the resulting tape length.

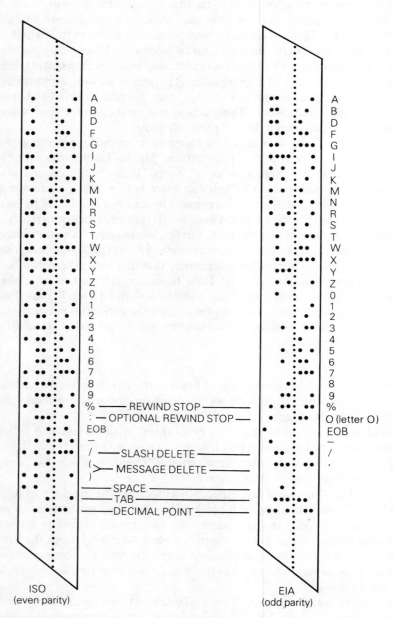

Figure 5.4 *Standard tape codes.*

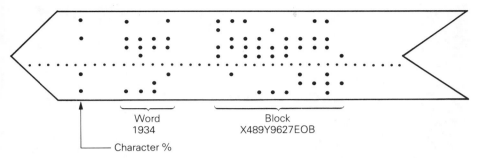

Word
1934

Block
X489Y9627EOB

Character %

Figure 5.5 *Perforated tape format.*

Production of punched tape   Punched tapes may be produced either from a teletypewriter or by an automatic tape punch interfaced (connected) with a computer. An automatic tape punch is shown in Figure 5.6.

The teletypewriter is similar in many ways to an electric typewriter. It has an alpha-numeric (letters and numbers) keyboard, and the pre-written program is typed in the normal way either on to conventional teletype paper or on to a blank program sheet. A teletypewriter is shown in Figure 5.7.

Attached to the side of the teletypewriter is the punching device. The blank tape feeds automatically from a roll into the punching head and, as each character is typed on the keyboard, a row of holes is punched in the tape.

Additional copies of the tape or of the typewrittten program can be made automatically.

The facility to produce additional copies can be used for tape correcting. The

Figure 5.6 *Automatic tape punch for interfacing with computer.*

Figure 5.7   *Teletypewriter used for production of perforated tape.*

original tape is run through the machine and while it is running through a replica of the tape and a printout are being made. At the point where the correction is to be made the automatic process is stopped. The new data are then typed into the program in the normal way. When the correction is completed the original tape is inched forward to the point where the original entry is still valid and the automatic reproduction process is restarted.

With computer-linked tape preparation facilities, editing is somewhat simpler. The listed part program appears on the display screen, where it can readily be examined, and any necessary alterations can be made via the keyboard. When the programmer is satisfied that all is correct the tape punch is activated to produce a complete new tape. Additional copies of the tape can readily be made and an interfaced printer will provide copies for filing for future reference.

Tape proving Before a punched tape can be used for machining it should be 'proved', that is, checked that the desired machine movements will be achieved. This can be done on the machine tool, although the wisdom of wasting valuable machining time in non-productive testing is questionable.

On basic numerically controlled machines, that is those not computer controlled, testing facilities are limited to a 'dry run', when the machine slide movements function but the spindle remains stationary. On computer controlled machines the dry run can be complemented by a 'test run', that is, all axis and spindle movement is inhibited but the visual display is continually updated as demanded by the program in real time, that is, the actual time it would take to machine the component. Errors in the program, e.g. no spindle speed stated, would be indicated by an appropriate error message appearing on the VDU screen.

Some control systems also have a 'check run' facility which is a rapid version of the test run.

To avoid incurring the non-productive down time referred to above, other test facilities remote from the machine may be more appropriate; for example a plotter may be used. A plotter is in effect an automatic drawing device. The profile of the cutter path is traced out by the machine according to the data supplied via the tape. The result is, of course, a 'flat' view; depth, that is, the third axis, is achieved by using colours. An interfaced printer may be used to provide a copy of the program and a drawing of the tool path.

The tape-proving facilities referred to above are largely redundant when computer graphics are used as part of the programming preparation process. The pre-prepared program is fed into the computer via keyboard, floppy disc or tape, the entry appearing on the visual display unit. Incorrect entries, for example an unrealistic feed rate, can be stalled and the operator informed by a displayed error message. When the program is complete it can be transferred to storage and the computer graphics are then used to simulate a test run. The correct blank size appears and, using animated tool movements, is 'machined' according to the program requirements. The use of a computer for program proving is illustrated in Figure 5.8. A computer printout of a program, together with a graphical representation of the component, is shown in Figure 5.9.

When the programmer is satisfied that the entry is correct a tape can be produced very rapidly at the touch of a key via an automatic tape punch interfaced with the computer. Similarly, an interfaced printer will produce a printout.

Magnetic tape data input

Magnetic tape, in the form of cassettes, is a widely used means of transmitting data. The advantages claimed for it are:

(a) easier handling;
(b) more rapidly produced and read;
(c) the program can be erased and the tape re-used;

Figure 5.8 **(a)** *Use of computer for program proving: program listing.*

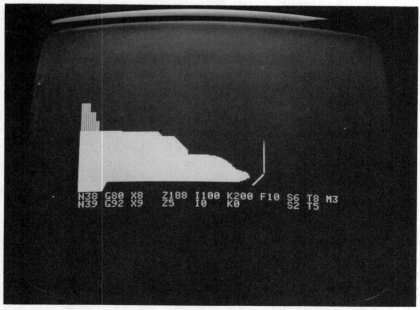

Figure 5.8 **(b)** *Use of computer for programme proving: graphical simulation.*

(d) simpler editing;

(e) more storage space than a paper tape of the same length;

(f) more durable than paper tapes.

Early applications of magnetic tape involved a recording being made as machining of the first component was being carried out 'manually' from the control console, a form of manual data input. A major drawback of this system was that the final program was only as rapid as the human reactions producing it and, with all the dial setting and switching involved, it was inevitably rather slow compared with modern techniques.

It was the advent of computer-controlled machining and computer-aided program proving that resulted in a more general application of magnetic tape. To record a part program in this way involves entering a program by MDI either at the machine control unit or through a computer keyboard. After the program has been entered it can be listed, edited and proved by using computer graphics, as discussed earlier. Finally the program is recorded in much the same way as a tape recording of a piece of music can be made from a record or the radio.

Magnetic tape recordings do have the disadvantage of not being visible, but in addition to displaying the program on a VDU they can also be used to drive a plotter, so providing such equipment is available this problem is readily overcome. It is also possible to get a printout of the program from an interfaced printer.

Magnetic disc data input

A relative newcomer to the recording and transmission of data for numerically controlled machines is the magnetic discette, commonly referred to as the 'floppy disc'.

Discs have the same disadvantage as magnetic tape in that the program is not visible, but as with tapes the program can be transferred to a computer for visual display and used to produce a printout or drive a plotter.

The rate at which data can be transferred or retrieved using a disc is much faster than when using a tape and, size for size, the storage capacity of the disc is much greater.

Master computer data input

The use of a master computer to input machining programs is a rather more complex process, and its application is dealt with more fully in Chapter 8. The prepared programs are stored in the memory of the computer and then transferred to the microcomputer of the machine control unit as and when required. A number of machining units will be involved, such an arrangement being referred to as direct numerical control (DNC). The concept is illustrated in Figure 5.10. The input of data to the master computer will be via keyboard, tape or disc.

Figure 5.9   *Computer printout and graphical representation of component.*

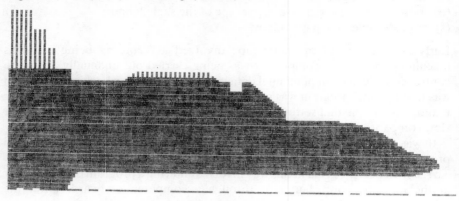

```
OPTIONAL STOP OUT.   SINGLE STEP OUT.


         TIME TAKEN - 11.93 MIN.
         ========================



PROGRAM USED TO GENERATE WORKPIECE
==================================

PROGRAM NUMBER 1
================


N1   G96                                    S1000
N2   G95
N3   G92 X10   Z0    I0    K1    F99 S9 T1 M8
N4   G82 X61   Z188 I61   K91            M3
N5   G81 X68   Z84  I68   K188           M6
N6   G84 X56   Z188 I56   K109           M3
N7       X51        I51   K114
N8       X46        I46   K119
N9   G0  X41
N10  G83       Z119 I45
```

```
N11 G81 X63   Z101  I63   K188
N12 G84 X36   Z188  I36   K159
N13     X31         I31   K165
N14     X27         I27   K170
N15 G82 X23         I23   K181
N16 G3  X29   Z167  I41
N17 G2  X41   Z139  I1    K139
N18 G80 X43   Z187  I16   K187
N19 G1  X22   Z181
N20 G3  X28   Z167  I42   K181
N21 G2  X40   Z139  I0    K139
N22 G83       Z119  I44   K119
N23     X60   Z103  I60   K90
N24     X65   Z85   I65   K45
N25 G0  X145  Z230
N26 G97
N27 G92 X10   Z0    I0    K0    F12 S3 T12M8
N29 G81 X0    Z153        K162             M3
N30           Z121        K130
N31           Z89         K98
N32           Z57         K66
N33           Z25         K200
N35 G92 X-11  Z0    I1    K0    F10 S6 T8 M8
N36 G82 X15   Z188  I15   K185             M3
N37 G3  X10   Z173  I49   K164
N38 G80 X8    Z188  I100  K200
N39 G92 X9    Z5    I0    K0        S2 T5
N40 G82 X62   Z95   I55   K95
N41 G4              I1000
N42 G80 X68         I68   K40
N43 G81 X60   Z40
N44 G85 X68   Z36   I60   K36
N45           Z31         K31
N46           Z27         K27
N47 G0        Z53
N48 G1  X60   Z45
N49 G80 X68   Z30   I100  K200
N50 G92 X5    Z3    I0    K1    F99 S5 T6
N51 G0  X66   Z100
N52 G34 X64   Z37         K50
N53     X63
N54     X62
N55 G0  X100  Z200                         M2
```

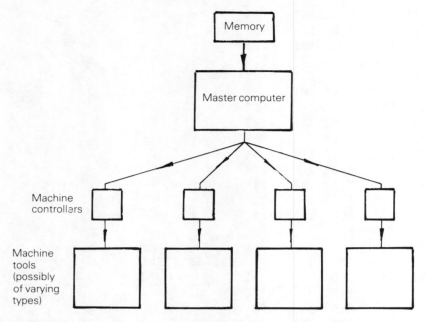

Figure 5.10   *Data input from master computer: direct numerical control (DNC).*

Buffer storage

Most modern control systems have a buffer storage, which is a capability to hold data extracted from the computer memory in an intermediate position. As one block of information is being processed the next is ready for instant transmission, the object being to speed the rate at which data are processed so that there is a minimum loss of machining time. Also, the elimination of a dwell between blocks avoids marking the machined surface.

QUESTIONS

1   When would it be economically inadvisable to enter data manually into a machine control unit?

2   What is conversational manual data input and what are the advantages and disadvantages of entering a machining program by this method?

3   Name three types of materials, or combinations of materials, used for perforated tape and state the advantages of each.

4   Name three types of tape readers. Which of these is most commonly used?

5   How is the reverse loading of perforated tape into a tape reader prevented?

6   Why is the binary system of numbers used to indicate the meaning of data input on a perforated tape?

7   What is the origin of the expression 'eight bit' as applied to perforated tape?

8   Name the two tape standards in general use and explain how, by a visual check, you could identify them.

9   Explain what is meant by 'character', 'word' and 'block' as applied to perforated tape format.

10   What is the difference between tab sequential and variable block tape format?

11   Describe two ways in which a tape can be proved away from the machine tool.

12   What is the difference between a dry run and a test run when checking data input?

13   What are the advantages of magnetic tape as a data storage medium?

14   What are the advantages of the floppy disc as a data storage medium?

15   What is a buffer storage and why is it necessary?

6

TERMS AND DEFINITIONS ASSOCIATED WITH PART PROGRAMMING AND MACHINE CONTROL

PART PROGRAMMING

The expression 'part programming' causes some confusion, since 'part' is often thought to mean something which is incomplete. In numerical control terms a part program is, in fact, a complete program. The word 'part' means component.

PREPARATORY FUNCTIONS

Preparatory functions are used to inform the machine control unit of the facilities required for the machining that is to be carried out. For example, the control unit will need to know if the axis movements stated dimensionally in the program are to be made in imperial or metric units, and whether the spindle is to rotate in a clockwise or counter-clockwise direction.

The way in which machine controllers are provided with such information depends on the type of control unit. On conversational MDI systems it may simply involve pressing the appropriate button on the control panel. For control systems using the word address method the various preparatory functions have been standardised (BS 3635:1972) and are commonly known as 'G codes', the address letter being G followed by two digits.

The standardised preparatory functions are shown in Table 6.1. Note that not all the possible code numbers are allocated, which means that control systems manufacturers can use those remaining for whatever purpose they wish. The codes used for programming will depend on the control system and the machine type. The codes available on any one system will be considerably fewer than those listed in the standard.

Many preparatory functions are modal, that is, they stay in operation until changed or cancelled.

Table 6.1 Preparatory functions codes (M = modal).

Code number	Function	
G00	Rapid positioning, point to point	(M)
G01	Positioning at controlled feed rate ⎫ Normal	(M)
G02	Circular interpolation ⎰ dimensions	(M)
G03	Circular interpolation CCW, normal dimensions	(M)
G04	Dwell for programmed duration	
G05	Hold. Cancelled by operator	
G06 ⎱	Reserved for future	
G07 ⎰	standardisation	
G08	Programmed slide acceleration	
G09	Programmed slide deceleration	
G10	Linear interpolation (long dimensions)	(M)
G11	Linear interpolation (short dimensions)	(M)
G12	3D interpolation	(M)
G13–G16	Axis selection	(M)
G17	XY plane selection	(M)
G18	ZX plane selection	(M)
G19	YZ plane selection	(M)
G20	Circular interpolation CW (long dimensions)	(M)
G21	Circular interpolation CW (short dimensions)	(M)
G22	Coupled motion positive	
G23	Coupled motion negative	
G24	Reserved for future standardisation	
G25–G29	Available for individual use	
G30	Circular interpolation CCW (long dimensions)	(M)
G31	Circular interpolation CCW (short dimensions)	(M)
G32	Reserved for future standardisation	
G33	Thread cutting, constant lead	(M)
G34	Thread cutting, increasing lead	(M)
G35	Thread cutting, decreasing lead	(M)
G36–G39	Available for individual use	
G40	Cutter compensation, cancel	(M)
G41	Cutter compensation, left	(M)
G42	Cutter compensation, right	(M)
G43	Cutter compensation, positive	
G44	Cutter compensation, negative	
G45	Cutter compensation +/+	
G46	Cutter compensation +/−	
G47	Cutter compensation −/−	
G48	Cutter compensation −/+	
G49	Cutter compensation 0/+	
G50	Cutter compensation 0/−	
G51	Cutter compensation +/0	
G52	Cutter compensation −/0	
G53	Linear shift cancel	(M)
G54	Linear shift X	(M)
G55	Linear shift Y	(M)

continued overleaf

Table 6.1—*contd.*

Code number	Function	
G56	Linear shift Z	(M)
G57	Linear shift XY	(M)
G58	Linear shift XZ	(M)
G59	Linear shift YZ	(M)
G60	Positioning exact 1	(M)
G61	Positioning exact 2	(M)
G62	Positioning fast	(M)
G63	Tapping	
G64	Change of rate	
G65–G79	Reserved for future standardisation	
G80	Fixed cycle cancel	(M)
G81–G89	Fixed cycles	(M)
G90–G99	Reserved for future standardisation	

MISCELLANEOUS FUNCTIONS

Apart from preparatory functions there are a number of other functions that are required from time to time throughout the machining program. For example, coolant may be required while metal cutting is actually under way, but will need to be turned off during a tool-changing sequence. Operations such as this are called 'miscellaneous functions'.

Conversational MDI control systems will, as with preparatory functions, have their own particular way of initiating miscellaneous functions, but for control systems using the word address technique the functions have been standardised (BS 3635:1972) and are commonly referred to as 'M functions', the address letter being M followed by two digits.

The standardised miscellaneous functions are listed in Table 6.2. The functions available will vary from one control system to another, the number available being fewer than the complete list.

POSITIONING CONTROL

The basis of numerically controlled machining is the programmed movement of the machine slides to predetermined positions. This positioning is described in three ways:

(a) point-to-point;
(b) line motion;
(c) contouring.

Point-to-point positioning
Point-to-point positioning involves programming instructions which only identify the next position required. The position may be reached by movement in

Table 6.2 Miscellaneous functions codes.

Code number	Function
M00	Program stop
M01	Optional stop
M02	End of program
M03	Spindle on CW
M04	Spindle on CCW
M05	Spindle off
M06	Tool change
M07	Coolant 2 on
M08	Coolant 1 on
M09	Coolant off
M10	Clamp slide
M11	Unclamp slide
M12	Reserved for future standardisation
M13	Spindle on CW, coolant on
M14	Spindle on CCW, coolant on
M15	Motion in the positive direction
M16	Motion in the negative direction
M17 M18	Reserved for future standardisation
M19	Oriented spindle stop
M20–M29	Available for individual use
M30	End of tape
M31	Interlock bypass
M32–M35	Constant cutting speed
M36	Feed range 1
M37	Feed range 2
M38	Spindle speed range 1
M39	Spindle speed range 2
M40–M45	Gear changes
M46–M49	Reserved for future standardisation
M50	Coolant 3 on
M51	Coolant 4 on
M52–M54	Reserved for future standardisation
M55	Linear tool shift, position 1
M56	Linear tool shift, position 2
M57–M59	Reserved for future standardisation
M60	Workpiece change
M61	Linear workpiece shift, position 1
M62	Linear workpiece shift, position 2
M63–M67	Reserved for future standardisation
M68	Clamp workpiece
M69	Unclamp workpiece
M70	Reserved for future standardisation
M71	Angular workpiece shift, position 1
M72	Angular workpiece shift, position 2
M73–M77	Reserved for future standardisation
M78	Clamp slide
M79	Unclamp slide
M80–M99	Reserved for future standardisation

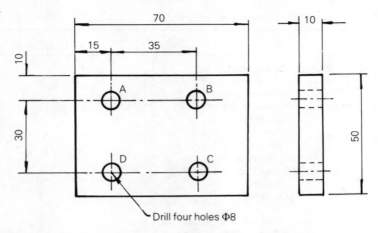

Figure 6.1 *Component detail involving point-to-point positioning.*

one or more axes. When more than one axis is involved the movements are not co-ordinated with each other, even though they may occur simultaneously. The rate of movement is usually, though not necessarily, the maximum for the machine.

Figure 6.1 shows a component the machining of which would involve point-to-point positioning, the holes being drilled in the sequence A to D. Note that it is the positioning prior to drilling that is point-to-point, not the drilling operation itself.

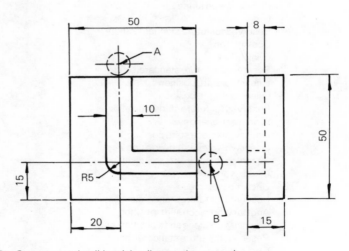

Figure 6.2 *Component detail involving line motion control.*

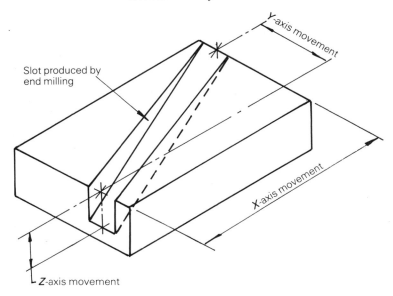

Figure 6.3   *Resulting tool path when three slides move simultaneously.*

Line motion control

Line motion control is also referred to as linear interpolation. The programmed movement results from instructions which specify the next required position and also the feed rate to be used to reach that position. This type of positioning would be involved in machining the slot in the component shown in Figure 6.2, the cutter moving in relation to the workpiece from point A to point B. Although a continuous cutter path appears to be the result, two distinct slide movements are involved, each slide movement being independent of the other.

Linear interpolation was initially defined as slide movement at programmed feed rates parallel to the machine axes. More recently it has also been used to describe linear movement when two, or sometimes three, slides are moving at the same time at programmed feed rates, a facility not available on earlier control systems. When two slides are moving simultaneously an angular tool path results, and when three slides are involved the result would be as indicated in Figure 6.3.

Contouring

Contouring also involves two or more controlled slide movements resulting from program data which specify the next position required and the required feed rates to reach that position, so there is some overlap between linear interpolation and contouring. However, contouring can also be much more

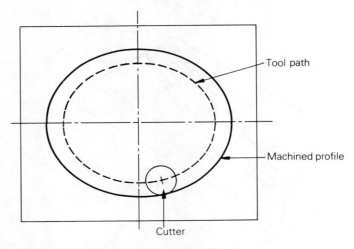

Figure 6.4 *Component profile produced by contouring.*

complex, involving combinations of angular movement and curves with one feature moving without interruption in the cutting process into another. This type of movement gives rise to the expression continuous path machining, which is often used to describe contouring.

Machining of the elliptical profile shown in Figure 6.4 would involve continuous path movement. Likewise the radii shown on the components in Figure 6.5 would be produced in a similar manner. The elliptical shape is not readily defined in numerical terms, and to produce the necessary cutter path would present an interesting, though not insurmountable, problem to the part programmer unless the control system was specially equipped with a canned cycle to deal with such a situation. On the other hand, the two radii shown in Figure 6.5 are an everyday occurrence and most control systems can readily accommodate the production of a radius, or a combination of radii. Such a facility is referred to as circular interpolation.

Circular arcs may be programmed in the *XY, XZ* and *YZ* planes. In exceptional cases three axes may be involved, resulting, in effect, in a helical tool path.

PROGRAMMING POSITIONAL MOVES

In practice the three types of positioning referred to above are rarely isolated. The production of the majority of components will involve a combination of the techniques. However, it will be necessary to clearly identify in the part program the type of positioning required at each stage of the machining process.

Manual data input systems will vary from one control system to another. For

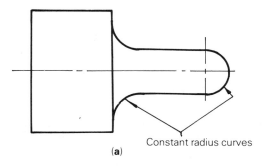

Constant radius curves

(a)

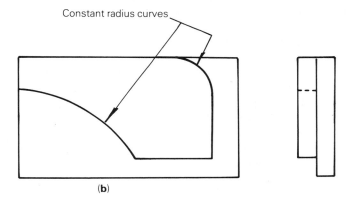

Constant radius curves

(b)

Figure 6.5 *Components with radial features requiring circular interpolation* **(a)** *turned compo-nent* **(b)** *milled profile.*

example, a widely used training machine specifies all linear movement as point-to-point and differentiates by linking the movement to an appropriate feed rate. The program entry is reduced to pressing a point-to-point key followed by the dimensional detail and the feed rate. Similarly, a radius is simply defined by pressing a circular interpolation key, followed by a data entry of the dimensional value of the radius and the direction of rotation as either clockwise or counter-clockwise.

Control systems using the recommendations contained in BS 3635:1972 will specify the type of positioning involved by using the appropriate preparatory function or G code, the common ones being as follows;

G00   Point-to-point
G01   Linear interpolation
G02   Circular interpolation clockwise
G03   Circular interpolation counter-clockwise

Having defined the type of positioning in this way the instruction is completed by including dimensional details of the move together with the feed rate for G01, G02 and G03. G00 moves are usually made at the maximum slide traverse rate for the machine.

DIMENSIONAL DEFINITION OF SLIDE MOVEMENT

In Chapter 1 it was explained that the axes in which slide movement can take place are designated by a letter and either a plus (+) or minus (−) sign to indicate the direction of movement. Unfortunately, these designated slide movements, owing to the different design configurations of machine tools, do not always coincide with the movement of the tool in relation to the work, and as a result this can cause some confusion when slide movements are being determined. In the case of a turning centre with a conventional tool post there is no problem, since the slide movement and the tool movement in relation to the work are identical. But on a vertical machining centre, for example, to achieve a positive (+) movement of the tool in relation to the work, the table, not the cutter, has to move, and this movement is in the opposite direction. Since a move in the wrong direction, especially at a rapid feed rate, could have disastrous results, this fact should be clearly understood.

A sound technique when determining slide movements is to program the tool movement in relation to the work. In other words, on all types of machine imagine it is the tool moving and not, as is sometimes the case, the workpiece. To do this it is necessary to redefine some, but not all, of the machine movements. A simple diagram such as the one alongside the components shown in Figures 6.6 and 6.9 is usually very helpful.

Once the direction of movement has been established it will need to be dimensionally defined. There are two methods used, and they are referred to as:

(a) absolute;
(b) incremental.

Figure 6.6 shows the profile of a component to be machined on a turning centre using the machine spindle centre line and the face of the workpiece as datums in the X and Z axes respectively. Assume the sequence of machining is to commence with the 35 mm diameter, followed by the 30 mm diameter and finishing with the 25 mm diameter.

To machine the profile using absolute dimensions it is necessary to relate all the slide movements to a pre-established datum. The movements required in absolute terms are indicated in Figure 6.7.

Incremental positioning involves relating the slide movement to the final position of the previous move. The slide movements, expressed in incremental terms, which would be necessary to machine the profile are indicated in Figure 6.8.

Note that each dimension in the X axis in Figure 6.7 is equal to the work

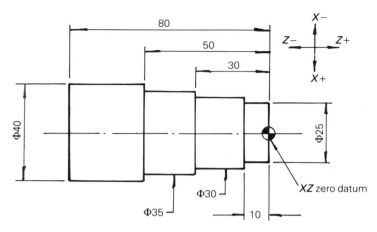

Figure 6.6   *Component detail.*

radius. Many control systems will require dimensions in the X axis when turning to be stated as a diameter, which is a more convenient method from a programming point of view.

Figure 6.9 shows a component which is to be milled in the sequence A to C on a vertical machining centre using datums as indicated. Assume that the movement in the Z axis to give a slot depth of 10 mm has already been made. The necessary slide movements in the X and Y axes in absolute and incremental terms are indicated in Figures 6.10 and 6.11 respectively.

CIRCULAR INTERPOLATION

It was stated earlier that circular arc programming on conversational MDI systems has been reduced to a few simple data entries. On control systems using the word address format it is rather more complex and there are slight variations in approach. Two of these variations will be considered later.

Common to all systems used to program circular movement is the need to determine whether the relative tool travel is in a clockwise (CW) or counter-clockwise (CCW) direction. The following approach is usually helpful.

1. For milling operations look along the machine spindle towards the surface being machined.
2. For turning operations look on to the top face of the cutting tool. (For inverted tooling this involves looking at the tool from below.)

The standard G codes for circular interpolation are G02 (CW) and G03 (CCW). However, not all systems adopt this recommendation and there is at least one widely used system in which they are reversed, that is, G02 is CCW and G03 is CW.

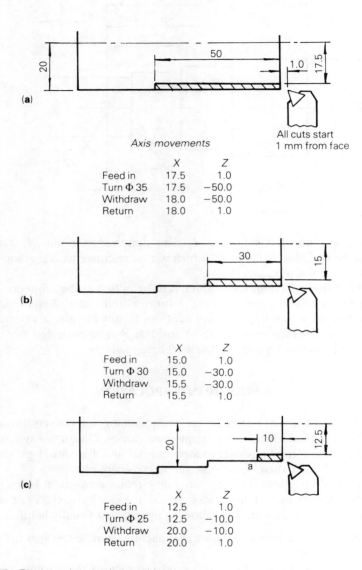

Figure 6.7 *Turning using absolute positioning.*

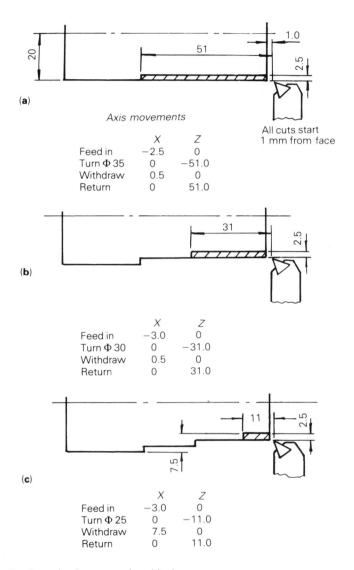

Figure 6.8 *Turning using incremental positioning.*

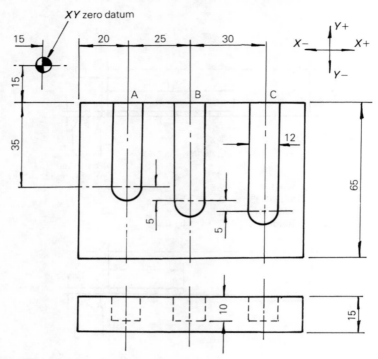

Figure 6.9   *Component detail.*

The two variations in arc programming referred to above are as follows.

Method 1

Assuming that the last programmed move brought the cutting tool to the start point, the arc is defined in the following manner:

1. The finish or target point of the arc is dimensionally defined in relation to the start point using the appropriate combination of X, Y and Z dimensional values stated in absolute or incremental terms.
2. The centre of the arc is dimensionally defined in relation to the start point using I, J and K values measured along the corresponding X, Y and Z axes respectively.

Thus the arc shown in Figure 6.12 would be programmed as follows. In absolute terms:

G 02	X	Z	I	K
	40	50	0	20

In incremental terms:

G 02	X	Z	I	K
	20	−20	0	20

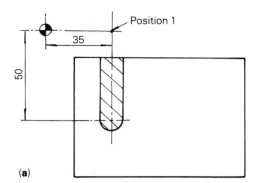

(a)

Figure 6.10 *Milling using absolute positioning.*

	Axis movements	
	X	Y
Move from datum to position 1	35.00	0
Mill to length	35.00	−50.00
Return to position 1	35.00	0

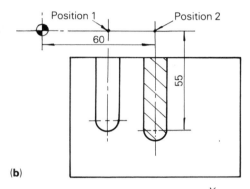

(b)

	X	Y
Move from position 1 to position 2	60.00	0
Mill to length	60.00	−55.00
Return to position 2	60.00	0

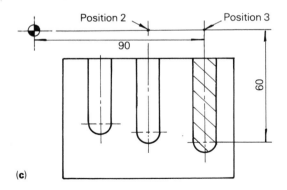

(c)

	X	Y
Move from position 2 to position 3	90.00	0
Mill to length	90.00	−60.00
Return to position 3	90.00	0
Return to datum	0	0

Figure 6.11 *Milling using incremental positioning.*

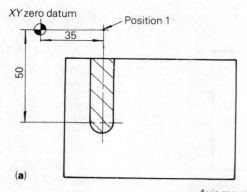

XY zero datum — Position 1

35

50

(a)

Axis movements

	X	Y
Move from datum to position 1	35.00	0
Mill to length	0	−50.00
Return to position 1	0	50.00

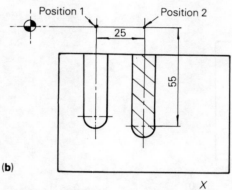

Position 1 — Position 2

25

55

(b)

	X	Y
Move from position 1 to position 2	25.00	0
Mill to length	0	−55.00
Return to position 2	0	55.00

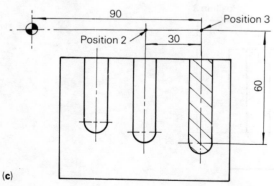

90

Position 3

Position 2 — 30

60

(c)

	X	Y
Move from position 2 to position 3	30.00	0
Mill to length	0	−60.00
Return to position 3	0	60.00
Return to datum	−90.00	0

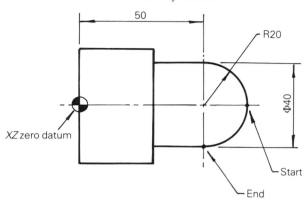

Figure 6.12 *Turned component detail involving arc programming.*

The variation in the X values in these two examples is because the absolute program assumes that X values are programmed as a diameter rather than a radius.

I has no value because the centre and start point of the arc are in line with each other. In practice, when a value is zero it is not entered in the program.

The I, J and K values are always positive.

Complete circles and semi-circles are programmed as a series of 90° quadrants. Thus a complete circle would require four lines of program entry.

Figure 6.13 shows the program for a milled profile. The cutter radius has been ignored.

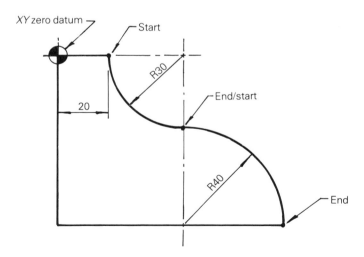

Figure 6.13 *Milled component involving arc programming.*

In absolute terms:

G	X	Y	I	J
03	50	−30	30	0
02	90	−70	0	40

In incremental terms:

G	X	Y	I	J
03	30	−30	30	0
02	40	−40	0	40

There are often situations where the start and/or stop points do not coincide with an *X*, *Y* or *Z* axis, and it is then necessary to make a series of calculations. Such a situation is shown in Figure 6.14. Dimensional values for *X*, *Y*, *I* and *J* have to be determined. The necessary trigonometry is indicated in Figure 6.15.

From A to B the magnitude of the *X* move is:

$$25.00 \text{ Cos } 30 - 25.00 \text{ Cos } 75$$
$$= 21.65 - 6.47 = 15.18$$

From *A* to *B* the magnitude of the *Y* move is:

$$25.00 \text{ Sin } 75 - 25.00 \text{ Sin } 30$$
$$= 24.15 - 12.50 = 11.65$$

The magnitude of the *I* dimension in the *X* axis is:

$$25.00 \text{ Cos } 75 = 6.47$$

The magnitude of *J* in the *Y* axis is:

$$25.00 \text{ Sin } 75 = 24.15$$

Once the dimensions have been determined they are incorporated in the program as before.

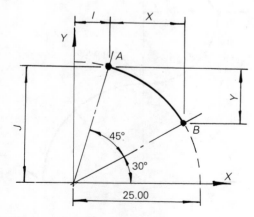

Figure 6.14 *Partial arc programming.*

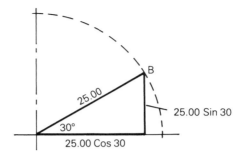

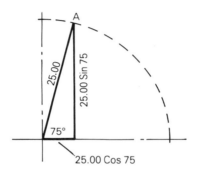

Figure 6.15 *Trigonometry required to program a partial arc.*

Method 2

The second method of arc programming varies from the one previously described in the way in which the arc centre is defined. As in the previous method, it will be assumed that the cutting tool has arrived at the start point of the curve. To continue, the following data are required.

1. The finish or target point of the arc is dimensionally defined in relation to the start point using the appropriate combination of X, Y and Z values stated in absolute or incremental terms.
2. The centre of the arc is dimensionally defined in relation to the program datum using I, J and K values measured along the corresponding X, Y and Z axes respectively.

Using this method the arc shown in Figure 6.12 would be programmed as follows.

In absolute terms:

G	X	Z	I	K
02	40	50	0	50

In incremental terms:

G	X	Z	I	K
02	20	−20	0	50

Note that in this example it is *I* that has no value, since the centre of the arc lies on the *X* datum and therefore *I* would be omitted from the program.

When the arc centre is related to the program datum it is possible for the *I*, *J* and *K* values to be a negative quantity, as illustrated in Figure 6.16.

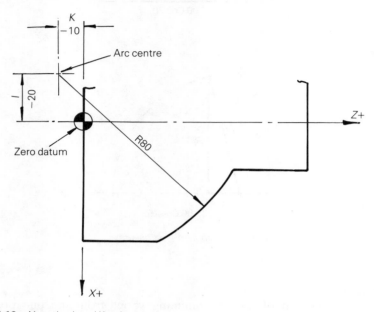

Figure 6.16   *Negative I and K values.*

RAMP

The starting and stopping of slide servo motors appear to be instantaneous. In fact there is, of course, a brief period of acceleration at the start of a move and a brief period of deceleration at the end of a move. This is shown graphically in Figure 6.17.

The period of acceleration is known as 'ramp up' and the period of deceleration as 'ramp down'. The ramp is a carefully designed feature of the servo motor.

From a metal-cutting point of view, the quicker a slide attains its correct feed rate the better, and ideally this should be maintained throughout the cut. The ramp period therefore is kept as brief as possible, but consideration has to be given to ensuring that at the end of the movement there is no motor over-run or

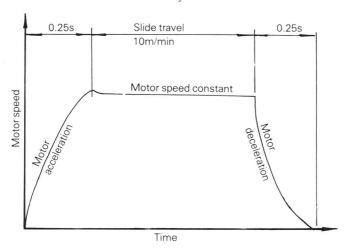

Figure 6.17 *Servo motor speed/feed rate relationship.*

oscillation, both of which could affect the dimensional accuracy of the component.

For linear interpolation the ramp effect is rarely of concern, but for circular interpolation, and particularly where one curve runs into another, it is preferable that there is no speed variation of the servo motor, and thus the feed rate of the slide, however small this might be. Any such variation would not only affect the metal-removal rate but may also affect the dimensional accuracy and surface finish of the component. Because of this, many control units are equipped with a *ramp inhibit* or *ramp suppression* facility, which means there is no slowing down or acceleration of the slide movement as one programmed movement leads into a second. G codes allocated to ramp are usually G08 and G09.

REPETITIVE MACHINING SEQUENCES

There are a number of machining sequences which are commonly used when machining a variety of components. Other less common sequences may be repetitive, but only on one particular component. It is helpful, since it reduces the program length, if such a sequence can be programmed just once and given an identity so that it can be called back into the main program as and when required. Such sequences are referred to in a variety of ways, for example as sub-routines, cycles, loops, patterns and macros. Although this can be slightly confusing, there are instances when one particular title appears to be more appropriate than the others. Various types of repeat machining sequences are discussed below.

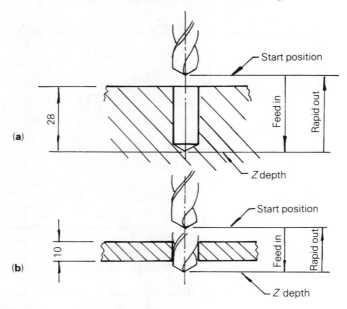

Figure 6.18 *Movements required to drill holes.*

Standardised fixed cycles

A number of the basic machining sequences commonly used have been standardised (BS 3635:1972) and are identified by assigned G codes. They are referred to as fixed cycles. Perhaps the most commonly used fixed cycle is that of drilling a hole. Consider the hole shown in Figure 6.18(a). The sequence of machine movements involved in drilling the hole would be.

1. Lower the spindle at a programmed feed rate.
2. Lift the spindle rapidly to the start position.

Now consider the process of drilling the hole shown in Figure 6.18(b). The same sequence of spindle movements is necessary; the only variation is in the depth of travel. To program such a sequence of moves is quite simple, but if there were a large number of holes to be drilled, apart from the boredom of repeating the necessary data when writing the program, the program itself would be very long. In addition, the fewer data that have to be handled the less likely it is that errors will be made. By standardising the sequence of moves the only additional data required are the length of travel, feed rate and spindle speed. This information, with the appropriate G code, is entered only once. Each time the slide moves to bring the spindle to a new position in relation to the work, another hole is drilled to the programmed depth.

Machining cycles involving linear movement that have been standardised are listed in Table 6.3.

Table 6.3 Standardised fixed cycles.

G code number	Movement in	At bottom		Movement out to feed start	Typical use
		Dwell	Spindle		
81[a]	Feed	–	–	Rapid	Drill Spot drill
82	Feed	Yes	–	Rapid	Drill Counterbore
83[a]	Intermittent	–	–	Rapid	Deep hole
84	Forward spindle feed	–	Reverse	Feed	Tap
85	Feed	–	–	Feed	Bore
86	Start spindle feed	–	Stop	Rapid	Bore
87	Start spindle feed	–	Stop	Manual	Bore
88	Start spindle feed	Yes	Stop	Manual	Bore
89	Feed	Yes	–	Feed	Bore

[a] See Figure 6.19.

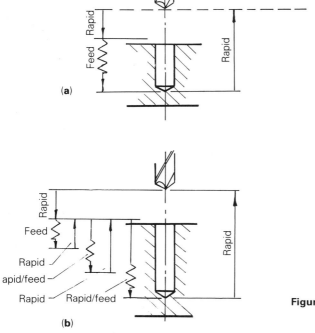

Figure 6.19 **(a)** *G81 drill cycle*
(b) *G83 peck drill cycle.*

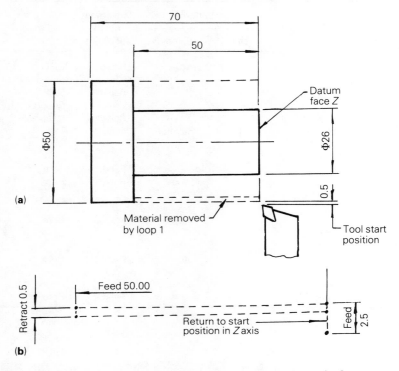

Figure 6.20 *Looping cycle* **(a)** *component detail* **(b)** *loop detail, repeated* ×6.

Non-standardised fixed cycles

BS 3635:1972 provides for the manufacturers of machine control units to include in their systems cycles which they deem to be appropriate. The cycles they include will depend on the machine type to which the control is fitted. Some of the more common cycles are discussed below.

Loops The term 'loop' is particularly relevant when reducing stock material to size by making a series of passing cuts. Consider the component shown in Figure 6.20, which is to be reduced from 50 mm diameter to 26 mm diameter by a series of cuts each of 2 mm depth. Assuming the starting point for the tool is as shown, the tool will first move in to a depth of 2.5 mm, thus taking a 2 mm depth of cut, travel along a length of 50 mm, retract 0.5 mm and return to the Z datum, so completing a loop. It will then move in a distance of 2.5 mm, feed along 50 mm, retract 0.5 mm and return to the Z datum, and so on. The loop, including the feed rate, is programmed just once, but is repeated via the 'loop count' data included in the main program as many times as necessary to reduce the work to the required diameter.

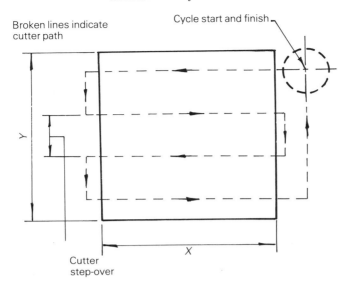

Figure 6.21 *Face milling cycle.*

Face milling cycle Figure 6.21 shows details of a face milling cycle. After programming the appropriate G code, together with spindle speed and feed rate, the only other information required is the X and Y dimensions of the face to be milled. The control unit computer will determine the number of passes necessary and the appropriate cutter step-over to machine the face.

Slot milling cycle Figure 6.22 illustrates a slot milling routine. As with face milling, the programmer has to state spindle speed, feed rate and the slot

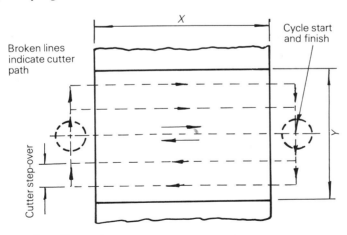

Figure 6.22 *Slot milling cycle.*

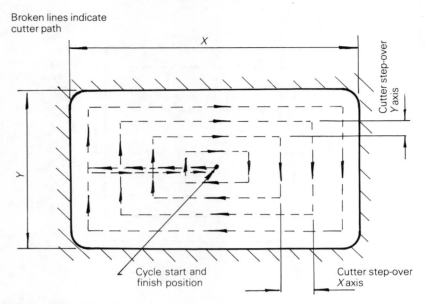

Figure 6.23   *Pocket milling cycle.*

dimensions in the *X* and *Y* axes. The first pass made by the cutter passes through the middle of the slot and then returns to the start. Further passes are made until the correct depth is achieved, the number of passes necessary being determined by the travel made in the *Z* axis before each cut commences, this increment also being part of the cycle data. When the correct depth is reached the cutter path is that of a series of loops increasing in size with each pass. Again, as with face milling, the computer will determine the step-over and the number of loops necessary to machine the slot to size.

Pocket milling   Figure 6.23 illustrates the pocket milling cycle. This cycle starts at the centre of the pocket, the cutter feeding in the *Z* axis to a programmed depth. There follows a series of loops until the programmed *X* and *Y* dimensions are reached, the step-over of up to 80 per cent of the cutter diameter to ensure that a perfectly flat surface is determined by the computer. Some systems provide for a cycle that roughs out the main pocket and then machines to size with a small finishing cut. If the pocket depth is such that more than one increment in the *Z* axis is necessary, the slide movement returns the cutter to the centre of the pocket and the cycle is repeated.

Bolt hole circles   The term 'bolt hole circle' means that a number of holes are required equally spaced on a stated pitch circle diameter as illustrated in Figure 6.24. Given that the program has brought the cutter to the pole position, the

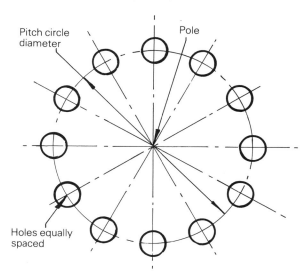

Pitch circle diameter

Pole

Holes equally spaced

Figure 6.24 *Bolt hole circle.*

other dimensional data required are the position of the first hole, Z axis movement, the pitch diameter or radius, depending on the control system, and the number of holes required. The computer makes all the necessary calculations to convert the polar co-ordinates to linear co-ordinates and to move the slides accordingly.

A variation of this cycle will cater for just two or three holes positioned in an angular relationship to one another. An example is detailed in Figure 6.25. Again, the pole position is programmed and the cutter will be at this point when the cycle commences. The additional dimensional data that have to be supplied are the Z axis movement, the polar radius and the polar angle(s), and the computer converts this information to slide movement in the appropriate axes.

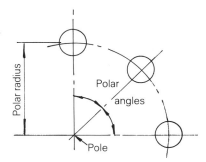

Polar radius

Polar angles

Pole

Figure 6.25 *Polar co-ordinates.*

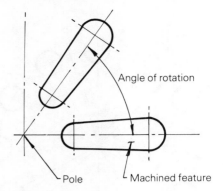

Angle of rotation

Pole   Machined feature

Figure 6.26 *Feature rotation.*

On some control systems it is possible to 'rotate' more complex features such as the example shown in Figure 6.26.

Cycles devised by the part programmer

While there are a number of machining sequences which are very common, there are other situations where sequences are repetitive, but only on one particular component. The component shown in Figure 6.27 has a repetitive feature, namely the recess. When writing the program for this component the necessary data for producing just one recess would be entered in the cycle file, a data page generally accommodating up to 99 program cycles. The cycle would be identified numerically and each time the main program reached the stage where the recess had to be machined all that would be necessary would be for the cycle to be recalled. It is also possible on many control systems to program cycles within cycles, a technique referred to as 'nesting'. Assume the component shown in Figure 6.27 to be quite large so that within each recess there were also a number of holes arranged in three groups, as shown in Figure 6.28. The main cycle would be the data necessary for the production of the recess, as explained above. The secondary cycle would be the data necessary to produce

Repetitive feature

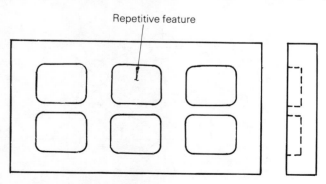

Figure 6.27 *Component with repetitive feature.*

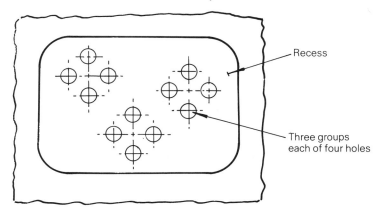

Figure 6.28 *Enlarged detail of component in Figure 6.27.*

a group of four holes. The secondary cycle would be nested within the main cycle and called into the main cycle program via its identity number, on three occasions.

However, the production of the four holes is repetitive, and thus it is possible to program to produce just one hole, but to repeat the sequence four times. The complete system of cycles for producing the component is illustrated diagrammatically in Figure 6.29. On some control systems it is possible to program cycles within cycles as many as eight deep.

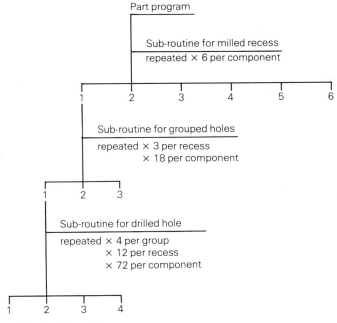

Figure 6.29 *'Nesting' three deep.*

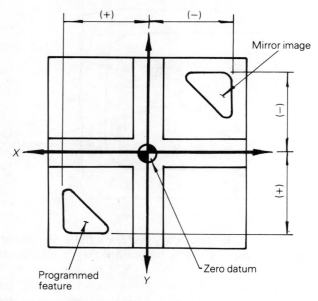

Figure 6.30 *Mirror image in two axes.*

MIRROR IMAGE

A commonly occurring aspect of mechanical engineering design is the need for components, or features of components, that are dimensionally identical but geometrically opposite either in two axes or in one axis. By using the mirror-image facility such components or features can be machined from just one set of data. The component shown in Figure 6.30 has a feature which is mirrored in two axes. Note that, to produce the second profile, the positive incremental values become negative and the negative incremental values become positive. To produce a feature of the opposite hand, as shown in Figure 6.31, the direction of slide movement changes in one axis only.

SCALING

Another common requirement in mechanical engineering design is components with the same geometrical shape but varying dimensionally. Figure 6.32 illustrates two such components. When a control system is fitted with a scaling facility it is possible to produce a range of components, varying in size, from one set of program data.

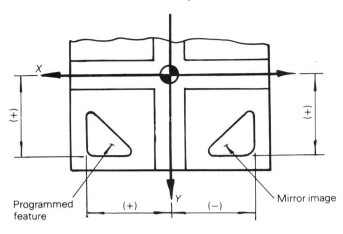

Figure 6.31 *Mirror image in one axis*

SLASH DELETE

The slash or block delete facility enables part, or parts, of a program to be omitted. It is particularly useful when producing components that have slight dimensional variations. For example, a hole may be required in one version of a component but not in another, although all other details may be identical. The program data relating to the production of the hole are contained within the programmed symbols /, one at the start of each block concerned and one at the end of the last block. An example is shown below.

N05 / G01　　Z1000 F 150*
N06 / G00　　Z-1000 / *

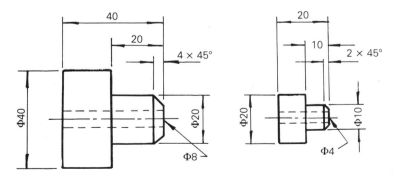

Figure 6.32 *Geometrically identical components suitable for production by scaling.*

To make a component *with* the hole the operator need not take any action. To produce a component *without* the hole the operator will have to activate the slash delete switch on the control console at the start of the program. When the first slash is reached the control unit will ignore the data that follow until the final slash is reached and then continue to execute the program. On some systems, if the slash delete is not activated the program will stop when the first slash is reached and the operator then has to make a positive response either to activate the data contained within the slashes or to delete them.

This facility is particularly useful when machining castings or forgings, where stock removal requirements may vary, the operator being given the option to include an extra cut or delete it as necessary.

JOG

The jog facility enables the machine operator to move the machine slides manually via the control console. This may need to be done for a variety of reasons, the most obvious one being when establishing datums at the initial setting of the machine. It may also be necessary to stop an automatic sequence and move the machine slides to facilitate work measurement, tool changing due to breakage, and so on. Whatever the reason, it is desirable that the automatic program is re-started at the point at which it was interrupted, and most control systems have a '*return from jog*' facility which returns the machine slides to their original positions, this facility being activated manually via a button on the control console.

PROGRAM STOP

Stops in a machining sequence can be predetermined and included in the part program as a miscellaneous function (M00). Scheduled stops for measurement, tool changing, etc. have to be notified to the machine operator so that he or she will be aware of his or her duties at this point.

Program stops can also be optional, that is, the sequence does not have to stop. Optional stops are also included in the part program as a miscellaneous function (M01) and the control will ignore the command unless the operator has previously activated a switch on the control console.

DATUMS

Base datum
The base datum, also referred to as a home datum, is a set position for the machine slides which places the cutting tool well away from the immediate

machining area to facilitate machine setting, tool changing or measurement of the workpiece.

Machine datum

The machine datum, also referred to as 'zero datum' or simply as 'zero', is a set position for the machine slides, having a numerical identity within the control system of zero. All slide movements are made in dimensional relationship to this datum as indicated earlier in the chapter, when absolute and incremental positioning moves were discussed.

On some machines the zero datum may be a permanent position which cannot be altered. On others a new zero is readily established by moving the slides so that the cutting tool is placed in the desired position in relation to the workpiece and then pressing the appropriate zero button on the control console. The facility to establish a datum in this manner is referred to as a floating zero or zero shift. The location of the original zero is not retained within the control memory.

A fixed machine datum may be helpful to the part programmer, especially when the programming is carried out remote from the machining facility, since the position can be taken into consideration when writing the program. It will be necessary, however, for the programmer to specify the exact location of the component in relation to the machine datum if the program is to achieve the desired results.

A floating zero affords greater flexibility when machine setting, since the work can be positioned anywhere within the range of slide movement and the zero established to suit. But this can be time-consuming and, if incorrectly carried out, may result in machining errors.

Program datum

The program datum or zero is established by the part programmer when writing the part program, and the program will require all slide movements to be made in relation to that point.

In practice, the machine zero and the program zero are often synchronised either by accurately positioning the work or, when possible, resetting the machine zero. Any unavoidable variations between the two positions can be accommodated by using the zero offset facility, if available, as described below.

ZERO OFFSET

The zero offset facility enables a machine zero datum to be readily repositioned on a temporary basis. Once it has been repositioned the slide movements which follow will be made in dimensional relationship to the new datum. It is particularly useful when the original machine datum does not coincide with the

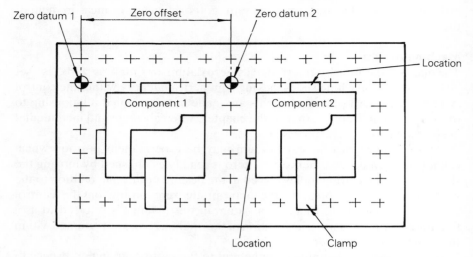

Figure 6.33 *The use of zero offset facility when machining components located on a grid plate.*

part program datum, a situation which can arise, for instance, when a part program has been prepared without regard to the normally fixed position of the machine datum and difficulties are encountered in positioning the workpiece to suit the part program. The zero offset facility also enables two or more components to be machined at one setting from the same part program. In Figure 6.33 component 1 would be machined with slide movements made in relation to datum 1. On completion of the machining sequence the machine table would be caused to move, via the part program or by manual intervention at the keyboard, by the predetermined offset dimension and the machining sequence would be repeated for component 2, with all slide movements being made in relation to datum 2. The control would retain information regarding the location of the original datum, which remains a permanent feature of the part program, and the machine slide can be caused to return to that position.

The facility may also be used to machine identical features on components of different lengths. A simple example would be to cut a screw thread of particular dimensions on the end of two bars the overall lengths of which are not the same.

On the more sophisticated controls it is possible to establish a new zero, or zeros, at various stages throughout the program. All subsequent moves will be made in relation to the new datum, but these moves are not necessarily a repeat of the moves made before the new zero was established. This facility enables the features of complex or very long components to be machined by relating slide movement to more than one datum, thus simplifying programming and possibly reducing machining time by limiting the length of slide travel.

QUESTIONS

1 What is a preparatory function and how is it designated in word address programming?

2 What is a miscellaneous function and how is it designated in word address programming?

3 What is meant by the term 'modal'?

4 Name and describe the three types of positioning control used on numerically controlled machine tools.

5 Explain, with the aid of a simple sketch, the difference between absolute and incremental dimension definition.

6 When are the letters I, J and K used in a word address program?

7 What do you understand by the term 'ramp suppression'?

8 Describe what happens during a peck drill cycle.

9 What is a looping cycle and when is it used?

10 Describe what happens during a pocket milling cycle.

11 What is a bolt hole circle?

12 What is meant by the 'rotation' of a machined feature?

13 With the aid of a simple sketch describe the effect of reproducing a machine feature using the mirror image programming facility in.
(a)   two axes;
(b)   one axis.

14 What is the programming function that permits the production from one set of data of components geometrically identical but with proportional dimensional variations?

15 Explain the meaning of the term 'nesting' as applied to machining cycles.

16 When is the block or slash delete facility likely to be used and how is it generally invoked?

17   What is the jog facility on a machine control system and when is it likely to be used?

18   Give two reasons for including an optional stop in a program.

19   Why is it necessary to inform a machine operator of the scheduled stops in a machining program?

20   With the aid of simple sketches describe the meaning of zero offset.

7

SPEEDS AND FEEDS FOR NUMERICALLY CONTROLLED MACHINING

It is difficult to determine precise data for any metal-cutting operation without knowledge of the practicalities involved. For example, the condition of the machine, the power available, the rigidity of tooling and work-holding arrangements, the volume of metal to be removed, the surface finish required and the type of coolant to be used are all factors which have to be given consideration. The data which follow are given as a guide only and to facilitate completion of the programming exercises in Chapter 8.

SURFACE CUTTING SPEEDS

The speeds in Table 7.1 are suitable for average metal-cutting conditions. In practice it may be possible to increase these speeds considerably for light finishing cuts or, conversely, to reduce them for roughing cuts.

Table 7.1 Surface cutting speeds (m/min).

Tool material	Part material			
	Mild steel	Cast iron	Alum. alloy	Brass
Cemented carbide	170	100	250	180
High-speed steel	28	18	120	75

SPINDLE SPEEDS

The surface cutting speed relates to the machine spindle speed as follows:

$$\text{Spindle speed (rev/min)} = \frac{1000 \times \text{Cutting speed (m/min)}}{\pi \times \text{Work or cutter diameter (mm)}}$$

Example. To determine the spindle speed required to turn 50 mm diameter brass using a cemented carbide tool and a surface cutting speed of 180 m/min.

$$\text{Spindle speed, rev/min} = \frac{1000 \times 180}{\pi \times 50}$$

$$= 1146$$

This spindle speed will be correct for turning 50 mm diameter bar. However, as the diameter decreases, as for instance during an end-facing operation, this spindle speed is no longer valid or efficient. On many numerical control systems it is possible to program a surface cutting speed only, and the machine spindle speed will automatically vary within the range of the machine to compensate for changes in the work diameter, thus providing a constant cutting speed.

MACHINING FEED RATES

The feed rate of a metal-cutting operation can be described as the speed at which the machine slide movements cause the cutting tool to penetrate into the workpiece. It is entered into a numerically controlled machining program either as millimetres per spindle revolution (mm/rev) or as millimetres per minute (mm/min).

The feed rates quoted in Tables 7.2, 7.3 and 7.4 for turning, milling and drilling common materials are for average metal-cutting conditions. In practice these rates may be reduced to improve surface finish or increased for roughing cuts.

Feed rates for turning

Cemented carbide tools are used extensively for turning operations. It is common practice for the manufacturers to quote recommended feed rates in millimetres per spindle revolution (mm/rev). Typical feed rates for different work materials are given in Table 7.2.

Table 7.2 Typical feed rates for turning (mm/rev).

Mild steel	Cast iron	Alum. alloy	Brass
0.25	0.25	0.3	0.3

To determine the feed rate in mm/min:

Feed (mm/min) = Feed (mm/rev) × Spindle speed (rev/min)

When a constant surface cutting speed is programmed, that is, the spindle speed varies automatically to compensate for variations in the work diameter, the feed rate is programmed in mm/rev to maintain a constant feed rate per spindle revolution. When the spindle speed is programmed at a constant rev/min the feed rate can be entered either as mm/rev or mm/min, since both will result in a constant relationship between surface cutting speed and feed.

Feed rates for milling

The manufacturers of milling cutters state recommended feed rates as mm/rev, mm/min or mm/tooth.

When feeds are quoted as mm/rev or mm/min they usually refer to specific cutters in the manufacturer's range and cannot be generally applied. For instance, if two face mills both of, say, 75 mm diameter, but one having five carbide inserts and the other six, were used at the same spindle speed with a feed quoted in mm/rev, it would mean that the cutter with the fewest teeth would be subjected to a much higher volume of metal removal per tooth than the cutter with more teeth. So for general use feed rates quoted in mm/tooth are more suitable. These data can then be used to determine the feed rate in mm/rev as follows.

$$\text{Feed (mm/rev)} = \text{Feed (mm/tooth)} \times \text{Number of teeth}$$

And from this.

$$\text{Feed (mm/min)} = \text{Feed (mm/rev)} \times \text{Spindle speed (rev/min)}$$

Typical feed rates are given in Table 7.3.

Table 7.3 Typical feed rates for milling (mm/tooth).

Work material	High-speed steel cutters		Cemented carbide cutters	
	Face and shell end mills	End mills and slot drills	Face and shell end mills	End mills [a]
Mild steel	0.25	0.15	0.30	0.18
Cast iron	0.30	0.18	0.50	0.21
Alum. alloy	0.40	0.17	0.60	0.25
Brass	0.35	0.15	0.40	0.19

[a] As with high-speed steel slot drills, the design of some cemented carbide end mills provides for both plunge and side cutting.

Feed rates for drilling

High-speed steel drills are used extensively for producing smaller holes. Since small-diameter drills are liable to break, the feed rate is related to the drill size. Typical feed rates are given in Table 7.4.

Table 7.4 Typical feed rates for high-speed steel drills

Drill size (mm)	2	4	6	8	10	12	14	16	18	20
Feed rate (mm/rev)	0.05	0.10	0.12	0.15	0.18	0.21	0.24	0.26	0.28	0.30

Cemented carbide drills, sometimes with tips brazed to a medium carbon steel shank, but more commonly as clamped inserts, are favoured for larger holes. The feed rates for these drills compare with those used for carbide insert end mills.

The feed rate for solid carbide drills can be determined only by experiment on the job in hand.

As with turning and milling, the feed in mm/rev can be used to determine the feed in mm/min, as follows:

$$\text{Feed (mm/min)} = \text{Feed (mm/rev)} \times \text{Spindle speed (rev/min)}$$

FEED RATE AND SPINDLE SPEED OVERRIDE

On the majority of control systems there are facilities which enable the operator to manually change, via a setting dial, both the feed rate and the spindle speed. Selection is usually on a percentage basis, 0 to 150 percent being fairly typical.

Changes in speed and feed may be necessary for a number of reasons. For example, the operator may judge that the rate of metal removal can be safely increased and so may increase the feed rate. Similarly, the operator may judge that a prolonged tool life would result if the spindle speed were decreased, or the surface finish being obtained from the programmed feed rate may be unsatisfactory, and so on. Manual control of speeds and feeds is also a very helpful feature when machine setting and program proving.

Changes made manually do not affect the basic program, although if an operator decides that the programmed feed rate or spindle speed for any part of a program is unsatisfactory he or she should make the fact known so that a permanent change can be made.

QUESTIONS

1 Select a suitable surface cutting speed and calculate the spindle speed required to turn a mild steel component with a diameter of 55 mm, using a cemented carbide indexable insert cutting tool.

2 If the component in question 1 has a second diameter of 24 mm, what change in spindle speed will be necessary?

3 Compare the surface speeds for machining mild steel using high-speed steel and cemented carbide cutters and express the variation as a percentage.

4 What do you understand by the term 'constant surface cutting speed'? Quote a situation where it may be desirable during a machining operation.

5 Select a suitable feed rate in mm/rev for finish turning free-cutting mild steel using a cemented carbide tool. Using these data, determine a suitable feed rate in mm/min for turning a diameter of 35 mm.

6 Select a suitable surface cutting speed and determine the spindle speed required to drill a 6 mm diameter hole in free-cutting brass.

7 Why is it that the feed rate in mm/rev for drilling operations varies with the drill diameter?

8 Calculate the approximate feed rate in mm/min for slot drilling brass with a high-speed steel cutter of 15 mm diameter.

9 Determine a suitable spindle speed for face milling aluminium alloy using a cemented carbide cartridge-type milling cutter of 100 mm diameter.

10 If the cutter in question 9 had six cartridges, what would a suitable feed rate be in mm/rev?

8

PART PROGRAMMING FOR NUMERICALLY CONTROLLED MACHINING

Whether a production scene incorporates total automation or merely one or two numerically controlled machines positioned among traditional machines yet to be discarded, at the heart of successful numerical control is efficient competent part programming. The practical *skill* level requirement on the shop floor is, without doubt, in decline, but a high level of practical *knowledge* is essential if part programmers are to use costly equipment at their disposal to the utmost advantage. The selection of a correct sequence of operations, together with efficient cutting speeds and feeds, tooling and work holding, and the ability to express these requirements in the correct format are of paramount importance.

Unfortunately, programming methods differ and even when the basic approach is similar (for example, word address, which is covered by BS3635:1972) there are still variations and peculiarities, and conversational manual data input is very individual.

Thus the reader should appreciate that the ability to program with one control system rarely means that knowledge can be used *in total* elsewhere. Specialist training is essential, and most machine-tool manufacturers respond to this by offering training courses as part of the overall package to customers buying their equipment. However, once the basic concepts involved in part programming are understood, the change from one system to another does not appear to be a major problem. Indeed, the variations encountered can be a source of much interest, while the mastery of yet another system can give considerable personal satisfaction.

DOCUMENTATION ASSOCIATED WITH PART PROGRAMMING

Before a part program can be compiled it is necessary to give some thought to the practical aspects of producing the component, and in most companies this is likely to involve the completion of an operation sheet. There is no standard

144

OPERATION SCHEDULE		PART No.		DESCRIPTION			SHEET No. OF
		MACHINE TYPE		COMPILED BY			DATE
OP No.	DESCRIPTION	TOOLING TYPE AND SIZE	WORK HOLDING	CUTTING SPEED	FEED RATE		SPINDLE SPEED

Figure 8.1 *Example of an operation schedule.*

operation sheet, and the format will vary from company to company. One which will meet the requirements of the exercises that follow is shown in Figure 8.1.

In addition to an operation sheet there is also the need for documentation relating to machine setting and tooling, because some of the decisions made during the operation planning stage, and which in turn are taken into account when writing the part program, are of direct concern to shopfloor personnel responsible for preparing the tooling and the machine. Again, there is no standard format for such documents. Each company will have its own procedure.

Information relating to work holding and datums is usually fairly straightforward. For example, the component shown in Exercise 1 could be held in a vice, using the corner of the vice jaw as a location point, and the part program would be written accordingly. This information could be stated by means of a single sketch on an appropriate form. Alternatively, the part could be located and clamped on a grid plate, in which case the programmer would convey to the shopfloor personnel the grid reference.

Information relating to tooling may be more complex, especially where pre-set tooling requiring replacement from time to time is involved. For example, consider a machine which uses tool holders such as that shown in Figure 8.2. Production of a component is likely to include a number of these holders all containing different tool types for different operations. The tool setter will need to know the tool type and the setting lengths. The machine setter will need to know the tool position in the turret. It may be helpful for both to know the operation for which the tool is intended. Information similar to this can be conveyed on a document such as the one shown in Figure 8.3.

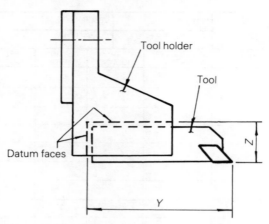

Figure 8.2 *Tool holder for turning operation.*

Another involved situation is when the precise sizes of the tooling to be used have not been stated by the programmer, their selection being left to the shopfloor personnel. The program will be written assuming that one tool will be set to the zero datum and all the other tools will be offset from that reference tool. As explained in Chapter 3, the operator will establish the offsets and enter their dimensional values in the offset file. The programmer, however, will require the various tools and offsets to be matched, and information of this nature will have to be supplied to the operator either on a suitable document or as part of the data input to the control unit being visually displayed on the VDU.

TOOL PREPARATION AND SETTING DATA				PART No.		
TURRET POSITION	OFFSET No.	OPERATION	INSERT TYPE	HOLDER TYPE	PRE-SET LENGTHS	
					X	Z

Figure 8.3

Finally, there is the documentation of the part program itself. Once again there is no standard form; there are as many different program sheets as there are machine control systems, although some similarity exists between documents used for word address programming. A program sheet suitable for entering word address programs is included at the end of the chapter. Note that a blank column is included for rarely occurring entries such as rewind stop or a time dwell.

PART PROGRAMMING PROCEDURE

The blocks of data entered in a part program are numbered N01, N02, N03, and so on. On completion of a machining program it is usually necessary to return to the beginning so that another component can be machined. The return to the program start position is usually achieved via a 'rewind' or 'return to start' command included at the end of the program.

With word address systems, this command is entered as a miscellaneous function designated M30, which has the effect of stopping all slide and spindle movement, turning off the coolant supply and rewinding the tape. When the tape has merely been used to transfer a program into the microcomputer memory, then it rewinds the program within the microcomputer. The stage at which this rewind must cease has to be identified, and this is achieved via a 'rewind stop' program entry signified by the % sign. This is usually the first entry in a word address program.

With the start of the program established, the next three or four blocks of data will concern setting the machine controller so that it interprets subsequent data in the correct manner. These set-up entries include instructions relating to the following:

(a) *units*, which may be programmed in metric or inches;
(b) *slide movement*, which may be stated as incremental or absolute dimensional values;
(c) *speed*, which may be programmed as surface speed in metres per minute or spindle speed in revolutions per minute;
(d) *feed*, which may be programmed as millimetres per spindle revolution or millimetres per minute.

Having established the basic set-up data, it is advisable now to list in a general way the functions and machine movements necessary to produce the component. Consider again the drawing for Exercise 1 and imagine that the machine is set with the spindle in its 'home' or 'base' datum position, that is, at a point some distance above the *XY* datum indicated on the drawing. Starting from this position, the part program must cater for the following:

1. Rapid linear movement to P1 in *X* and *Y*.
2. Rapid linear movement to *Z*0.

3. Spindle on clockwise direction.
4. Coolant on.
5. Feed linear movement to Z depth.
6. Rapid linear movement to Z0.
7. Rapid linear movement to P2.
8. Feed linear movement to Z depth.
9. Rapid linear movement to Z0.
. . . and so on.

These simple comments can be entered directly on to a program sheet, but it is probably a better plan to prepare a rough list in the first instance and then check carefully to ensure nothing has been overlooked. Relative codes and data can then be added to each statement.

Should it be found that, on completion of a program, omissions have inadvertently been made, the error can be rectified more easily if the block numbers are allocated in increments of five: N01, N05, N10, N15. It is then a simple matter to include additional blocks—N06, N07, N08, for instance—between N05 and N10.

If the program is being listed on a computer the blocks can be numbered consecutively, since any omission entered via the keyboard will automatically cause the existing blocks to renumber. Many MDI control systems also have this facility.

A methodical approach to part programming is essential, and it is recommended that, even for a simple component, an operation schedule listing the tooling speeds and feeds to be used should be completed in the first instance.

PROGRAMMING EXERCISES

Ideally, any part programming exercise should be supported by program proving and production of the component. Most of the exercises which follow will fall within the capacity of equipment now generally available in educational institutions, and it is likely that most benefit will be gained if the exercises are completed with that equipment in mind.

To cater for students who do not have access to suitable equipment two imaginary machine types, together with their control systems, are included on pages 166 to 172. These alternative systems are fairly typical and are illustrative of the way manufactureres summarise the capabilities of machines and control systems in their promotional literature and instruction manuals.

It is anticipated, if the exercises are attempted using the alternative systems, that, as when using college-based equipment, the student will receive further guidance and advice from his or her lecturer. Partially completed programs for Exercises 1, 2, 9 and 10 are included at the end of the chapter.

Details of the machining, tooling and programming requirements are included alongside each detail drawing with the exception of the last exercise of each type, where the intention is that the student should complete all stages from detail drawing to finished product, making decisions relating to work holding, tooling, feeds and speeds followed by part programming and, in cases where the programming has been related to equipment available, by program proving and final machining.

Appropriate speeds and feeds may be selected from the data given in Chapter 7.

The components have been dimensioned according to traditional standards in some cases, and in others the method of dimensioning which is increasingly being favoured for numerical control is used. Students will be able to judge for themselves which is the more appropriate.

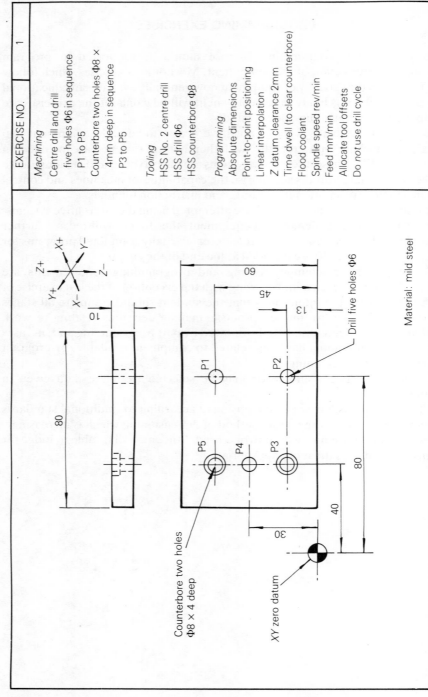

Machining

Centre drill and drill
five holes Φ6 in sequence
P1 to P5

Counterbore two holes Φ8 ×
4mm deep in sequence
P3 to P5

Tooling

HSS No. 2 centre drill
HSS drill Φ6
HSS counterbore Φ8

Programming

Absolute dimensions
Point-to-point positioning
Linear interpolation
Z datum clearance 2mm
Time dwell (to clear counterbore)
Flood coolant
Spindle speed rev/min
Feed mm/min
Allocate tool offsets
Do *not* use drill cycle

Drill five holes Φ6

Counterbore two holes
Φ8 × 4 deep

XY zero datum

Material: mild steel

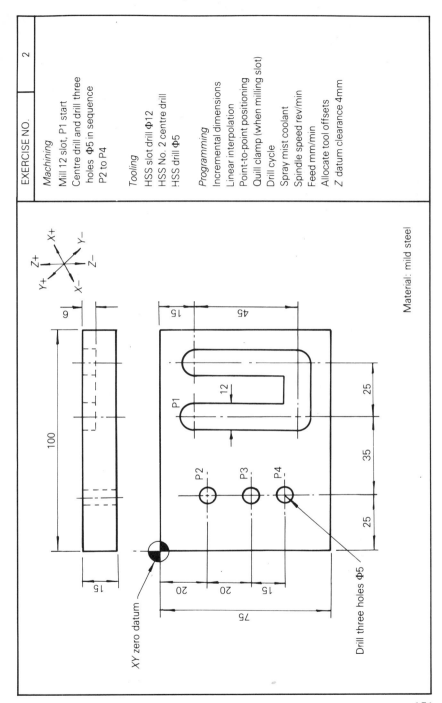

Machining

Mill 12 slot, P1 start
Centre drill and drill three
holes Φ5 in sequence
P2 to P4

Tooling

HSS slot drill Φ12
HSS No. 2 centre drill
HSS drill Φ5

Programming

Incremental dimensions
Linear interpolation
Point-to-point positioning
Quill clamp (when milling slot)
Drill cycle
Spray mist coolant
Spindle speed rev/min
Feed mm/min
Allocate tool offsets
Z datum clearance 4mm

Material: mild steel

Drill three holes Φ5

XY zero datum

151

EXERCISE NO.	3

Machining

Mill 8mm step in two passes
Centre drill and drill four holes
Φ5 sequence P1 to P4

Tooling

Tungsten carbide insert end mill,
Φ15, four teeth
HSS No. 2 centre drill
HSS drill Φ8

Programming

Absolute dimensions
Linear interpolation
Point-to-point positioning
Cutter compensation
Quill clamp (when milling steps)
Flood coolant
Drill cycle
Spindle speed rev/min
Feed mm/min
Allocate tool offsets
Z datum clearance 2mm

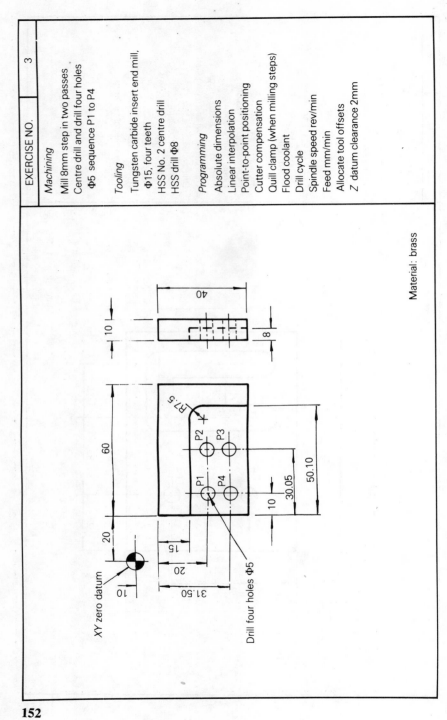

XY zero datum

Drill four holes Φ5

Material: brass

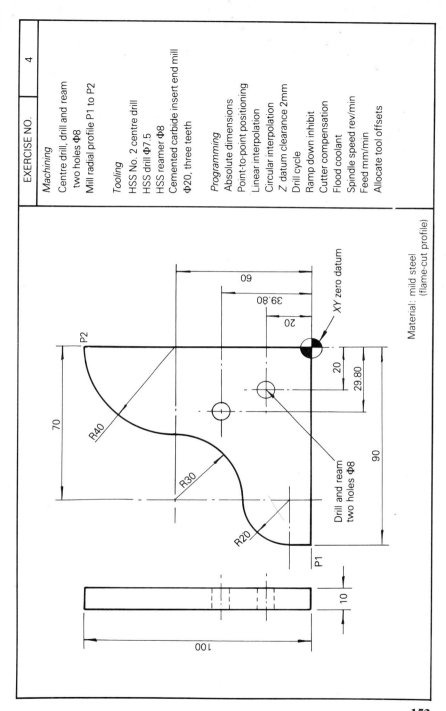

EXERCISE NO.	4

Machining

Centre drill, drill and ream
two holes Φ8
Mill radial profile P1 to P2

Tooling

HSS No. 2 centre drill
HSS drill Φ7.5
HSS reamer Φ8
Cemented carbide insert end mill
Φ20, three teeth

Programming

Absolute dimensions
Point-to-point positioning
Linear interpolation
Circular interpolation
Z datum clearance 2mm
Drill cycle
Ramp down inhibit
Cutter compensation
Flood coolant
Spindle speed rev/min
Feed mm/min
Allocate tool offsets

Material: mild steel
(flame-cut profile)

153

Machining

Drill and ream Φ15 hole
Rough mill corners and finish profile
with continuous cut P1 to P6

Tooling

HSS No. 3 centre drill
HSS drill Φ8
HSS drill Φ14.5
HSS reamer Φ15
Cemented carbide insert end mill
Φ12, three teeth

Programming

Absolute dimensions
Z datum clearance 2 mm
Linear interpolation
Circular interpolation
Cutter compensation
Spray mist coolant
Spindle speed rev/min
Feed mm/rev
Allocate tool offsets

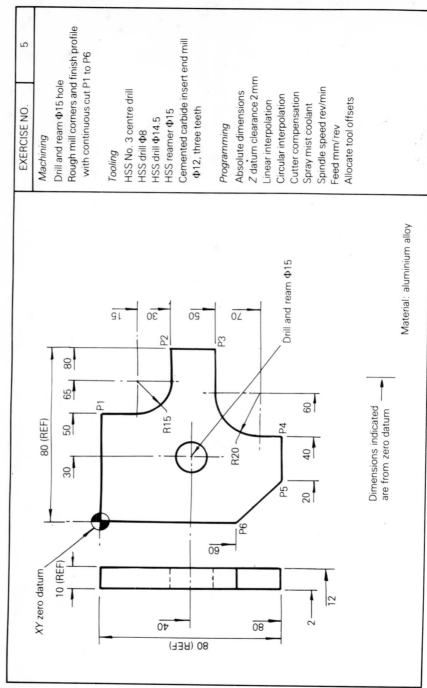

Material: aluminium alloy

154

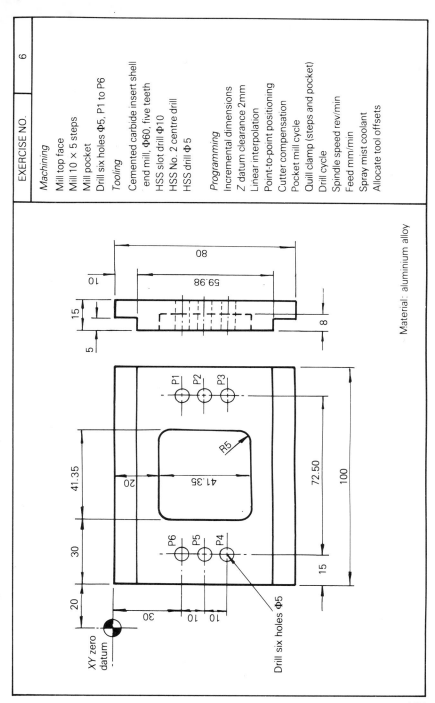

EXERCISE NO.	6

Machining
Mill top face
Mill 10 × 5 steps
Mill pocket
Drill six holes Φ5, P1 to P6

Tooling
Cemented carbide insert shell
end mill, Φ60, five teeth
HSS slot drill Φ10
HSS No. 2 centre drill
HSS drill Φ5

Programming
Incremental dimensions
Z datum clearance 2mm
Linear interpolation
Point-to-point positioning
Cutter compensation
Pocket mill cycle
Quill clamp (steps and pocket)
Drill cycle
Spindle speed rev/min
Feed mm/min
Spray mist coolant
Allocate tool offsets

Material: aluminium alloy

155

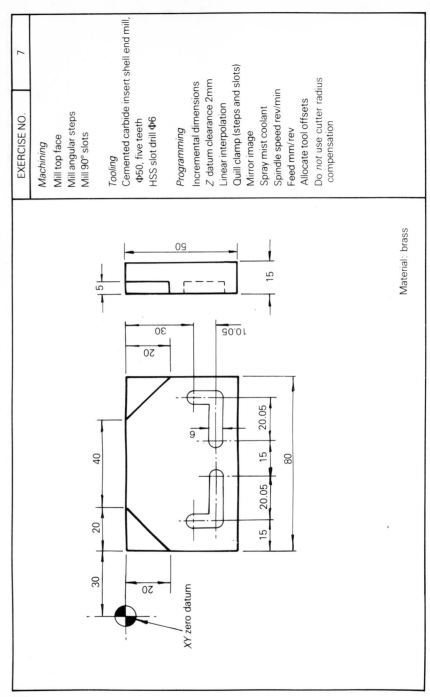

Machining

Mill top face
Mill angular steps
Mill 90° slots

Tooling

Cemented carbide insert shell end mill,
Φ50, five teeth
HSS slot drill Φ6

Programming

Incremental dimensions
Z datum clearance 2mm
Linear interpolation
Quill clamp (steps and slots)
Mirror image
Spray mist coolant
Spindle speed rev/min
Feed mm/rev
Allocate tool offsets
Do *not* use cutter radius
compensation

50

5

15

30

20

40

20

30

20

10.05

20.05

15

6

20.05

15

80

XY zero datum

Material: brass

156

Machining

Material supplied pre-machined
20 × 80 × 80

All other features to be machined

Complete an operation schedule
(see Figure 8.1)

Detail tooling to be used

Detail work-holding and
setting arrangements

Determine appropriate speeds
and feeds

Complete a part program

Prove the part program

Machine the component

(Note: Z datum clearance 4mm)

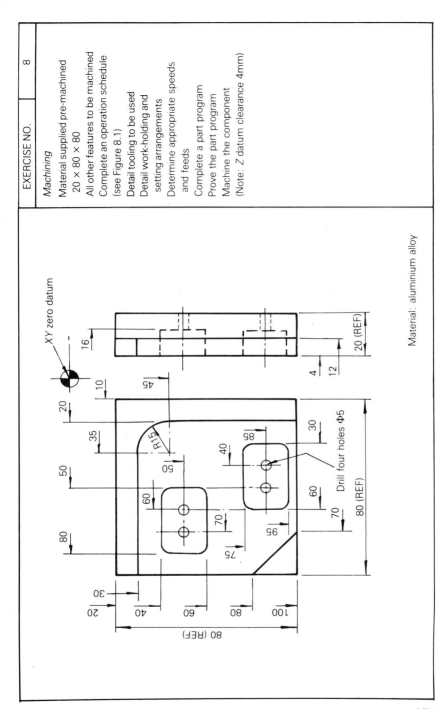

Drill four holes Φ5

Material: aluminium alloy

157

EXERCISE NO.	9

Machining

Stock material Φ50, hand loaded
and positioned
Face one end
Turn Φ45, Φ35 and Φ25, two
passes per diameter
Part off to length

Tooling

Light turning and facing,
cemented carbide insert
Parting off, cemented carbide
insert 3mm wide

Programming

Absolute positioning
Linear interpolation
Feed mm/rev
Spindle speed rev/min
Spray mist coolant
Allocate tool offset numbers
Ignore tool-tip radius

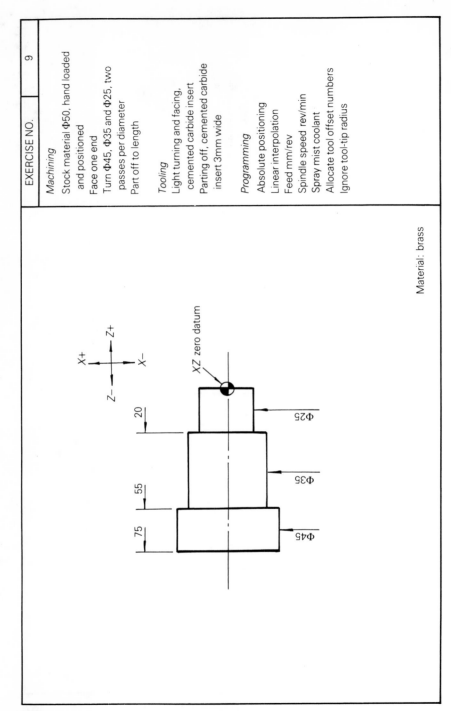

Material: brass

Machining

Material pre-faced billet Φ100,
hand loaded and located against
back face of chuck
Face second end to length
Centre drill
Drill Φ20 in two stages
Bore Φ40, Φ60 and Φ80
Depth of cut 2mm per pass

Tooling

No. 3 HSS centre drill
HSS drill Φ10
HSS drill Φ20
Internal turning tool, cemented
carbide insert
Facing tool, cemented carbide insert

Programming

Absolute dimensions
Linear interpolation
Feed mm/rev
Surface cutting speed m/min
Ignore tool-tip radius
Allocate offset numbers
Flood coolant

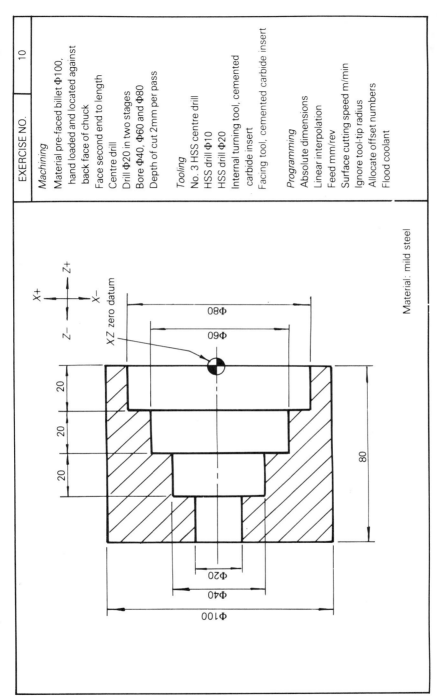

Material: mild steel

159

EXERCISE NO.	11

Machining

Stock material Φ40 hand loaded
and positioned
Face one end
Centre drill
Drill Φ4 hole
Rough turn to profile
Finish turn with continuous cut
Part off

Tooling

Light turning and facing tool,
cemented carbide insert
HSS No. 2 centre drill
HSS drill Φ4
Parting-off tool, cemented carbide
insert 3mm wide

Programming

Absolute dimensions
Linear interpolation
Feed mm/rev varied for roughing and
finishing cuts
Surface cutting speed m/min varied
for roughing and finishing cuts
Flood coolant
Peck drill cycle
Ignore tool-tip radius
Allocate tool offset numbers

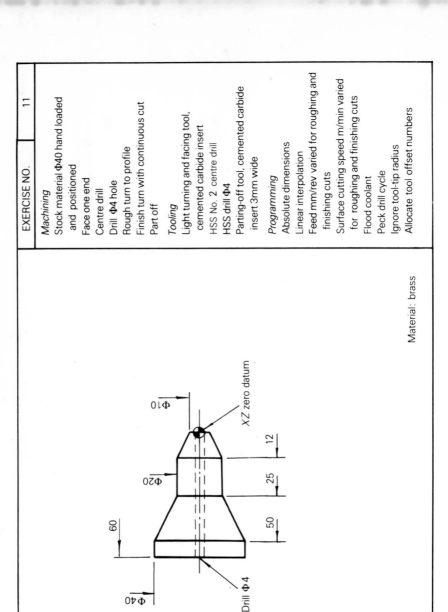

Material: brass

EXERCISE NO.	12

Machining

Material pre-faced billet Φ70 hand
loaded and located against
back face of chuck
Face second end to length
Centre drill
Drill in two stages
Ream
Rough turn to profile
Finish turn profile

Tooling

Light turning and facing tool, cemented
carbide insert, tip radius 2.0mm
HSS No. 3 centre drill
HSS drill Φ6
HSS drill Φ11.5
HSS reamer Φ12

Programming

Absolute dimensions
Linear interpolation
Circular interpolation
Cutter radius compensation
Feed mm/rev, varied for roughing and
finishing cuts
Surface cutting speed m/min varied
for roughing and finishing cuts
Mist coolant
Peck drill cycle for initial drilling
Allocate tool offset numbers

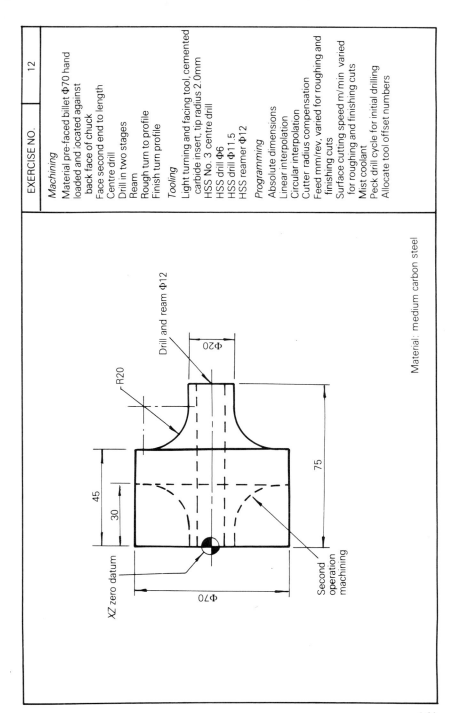

Drill and ream Φ12

R20

Φ20

45

30

75

Φ70

XZ zero datum

Second
operation
machining

Material: medium carbon steel

161

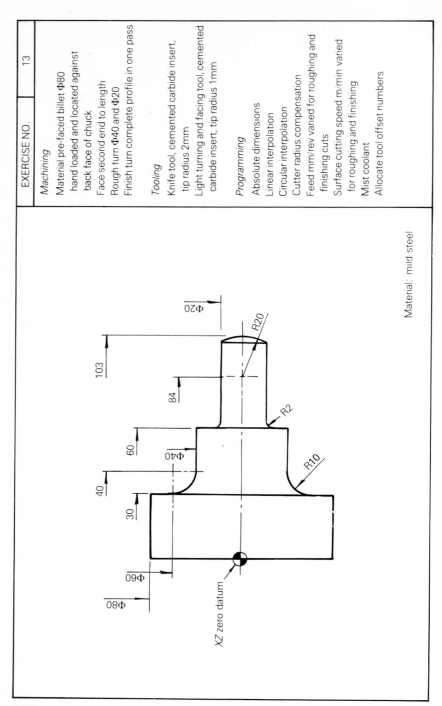

EXERCISE NO.	13

Machining

Material pre-faced billet Φ80
hand loaded and located against
back face of chuck
Face second end to length
Rough turn Φ40 and Φ20
Finish turn complete profile in one pass

Tooling

Knife tool, cemented carbide insert,
tip radius 2mm
Light turning and facing tool, cemented
carbide insert, tip radius 1mm

Programming

Absolute dimensions
Linear interpolation
Circular interpolation
Cutter radius compensation
Feed mm/rev varied for roughing and
finishing cuts
Surface cutting speed m/min varied
for roughing and finishing
Mist coolant
Allocate tool offset numbers

Material: mild steel

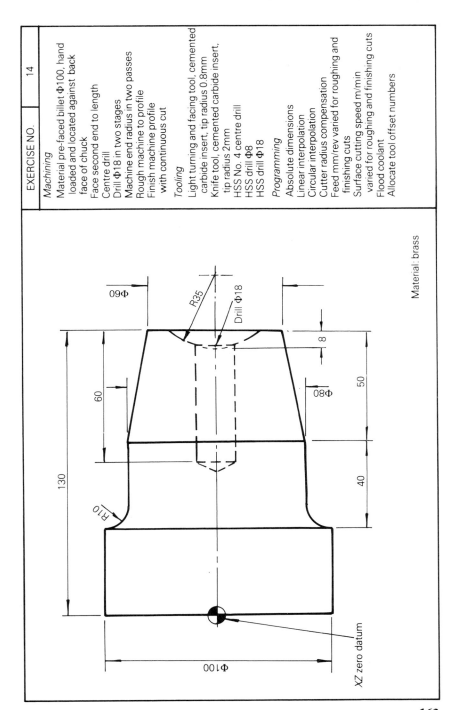

EXERCISE NO.	14

Machining

Material pre-faced billet Φ100, hand
 loaded and located against back
 face of chuck
Face second end to length
Centre drill
Drill Φ18 in two stages
Machine end radius in two passes
Rough machine to profile
Finish machine profile
 with continuous cut

Tooling

Light turning and facing tool, cemented
 carbide insert, tip radius 0.8mm
Knife tool, cemented carbide insert,
 tip radius 2mm
HSS No. 4 centre drill
HSS drill Φ8
HSS drill Φ18

Programming

Absolute dimensions
Linear interpolation
Circular interpolation
Cutter radius compensation
Feed mm/rev varied for roughing and
 finishing cuts
Surface cutting speed m/min
 varied for roughing and finishing cuts
Flood coolant
Allocate tool offset numbers

Material: brass

163

EXERCISE NO.	15

Machining

Stock material Φ40, hand loaded
 and positioned
Face end
Turn Φ38, Φ30, Φ25
Screw cut M30 × 1
Centre drill
Drill Φ8
Part off to length

Tooling

Light turning and facing tool, cemented
 carbide insert, tip radius 0.5mm
Grooving tool, cemented carbide
 insert, 5mm wide
Parting-off tool, cemented carbide
 insert, 3mm wide
Screw cutting tool, cemented
 carbide insert, metric form

Programming

Absolute positioning
Linear interpolation
Circular interpolation
Cutter radius compensation
Screw cutting cycle
Peck drilling cycle
Feed mm/rev
Surface cutting speed m/min
No coolant
Allocate tool offsets

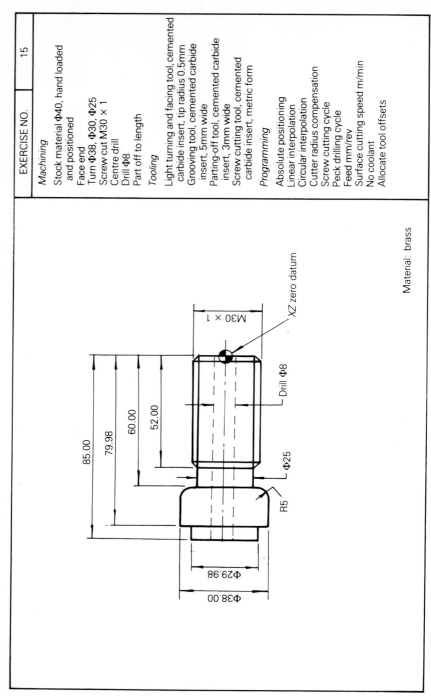

Material: brass

Machining

Material pre-faced billet Φ80.

Machine to drawing

Complete an operation schedule
(see Figure 8.1)

Detail tooling to be used

Detail work-holding and
setting arrangements

Determine appropriate speeds
and feeds

Complete a part program

Prove the part program

Machine the component

(Note: Z datum clearance 4mm)

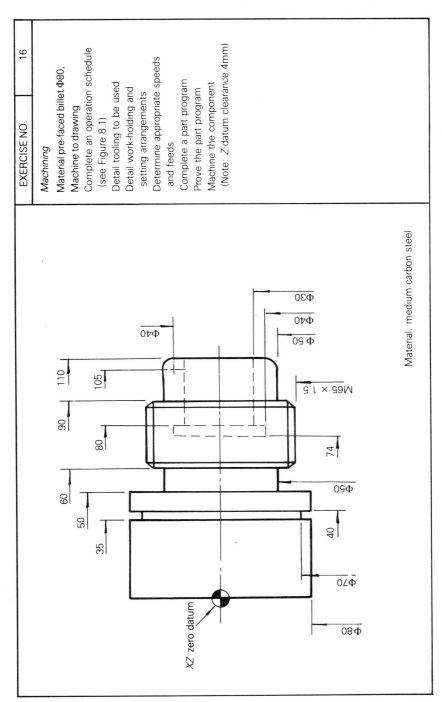

Material: medium carbon steel

ALTERNATIVE MACHINE SPECIFICATION AND CONTROL SYSTEM FOR PROGRAMMING EXERCISES 1 TO 8: MILLING AND DRILLING

Machine type and specification

Vertical machining centre with three-axis control

Traverse:	*X* longitudinal 600 mm (24 in.)
	Y transverse 400 mm (16 in.)
	Z vertical 450 mm (18 in.)
Spindle speed:	10–3300 rev/min infinitely variable
Working surface:	1000 mm × 300 mm (40 in. × 12 in.)
Feeds:	1–5000 mm/min (0.1–198 in/min)
Tool changing:	Manual

Control system

Program format:	Word address
Axes controlled:	*X, Y* and *Z* singly or simultaneously
Interpolation:	Linear *X, Y* and *Z*
	Circular *XY, YZ* and *ZX* planes
Command system:	Incremental or absolute
Data input:	MDI or perforated eight-track tape
Tape code:	ISO or EIA via tape sensing

Programming information

Block numbers:	N plus one to three digits
Preparatory functions:	G plus two digits
G00	Rapid traverse at machine maximum (modal)
G01	Linear interpolation, programmed feed (modal)
G02	Clockwise circular interpolation (modal)
G03	Counter-clockwise circular interpolation (modal)
G08	Ramp down inhibit (modal) (see p. 122)
G09	Cancels G08
G28	Pocket clearance cycle (modal) (see p. 168)
G30	Cancels mirror image
G31	Mirror image with axis command (modal) (see p. 168)
G40	Cutter offset cancel
G41	Cutter radius compensation left (modal)
G42	Cutter radius compensation right (modal)
G70	Inch programming (modal)
G71	Metric programming (modal)
G80	Cancels all fixed cycles
G81	Drill cycle (modal)
G83	Peck drill cycle (modal)
G90	Absolute programming (modal)
G91	Incremental programming (modal)
G93	Feed mm/min (modal)
G94	Feed in./min (modal)
G95	Feed mm/rev (modal)
G96	Feed in./rev (modal)
G97	Spindle speed rev/min (modal)

G02, G03 — (see pp. 113–121)

G41, G42 — (see p. 168)

G81, G83 — (see p. 168)

Assigned miscellaneous functions: M plus two digits

M00	Programmed stop. Stops all slide movement, spindle rotation and coolant
M01	Optional stop. Ignored unless activated manually from control console.
M02	End of program
M03	Spindle on clockwise
M04	Spindle on counter-clockwise
M05	Spindle off
M07	Coolant on (mist)
M08	Coolant on (flood)
M09	Coolant off
M10	Quill clamp on
M11	Quill clamp off
M30	End of program. Rewind tape.

Axis movement commands:	End point in X, Y and Z
	Start point of arcs relative to circle centre I, J and K (see pp. 113–121)
	Dimensional values in 3/2 format, that is, three digits before and two digits after the decimal point. Do not program the decimal point and omit leading zeros.
	Plus (+) signs are not required but (−) signs must be included.

Other functions:

Feed	F plus four digits
	Feed/min in 1 mm or 0.1 in. steps
	Feed/rev in 0.001 mm or 0.001 in. steps
	Do not program decimal point or leading zeros
Spindle speed	S plus four digits
Tool identification	T plus two digits
	T01 to T16. With offsets plus four digits, offsets 00 to 32.
Dwell	D plus three digits in 0.1 s. (Do not program decimal point.)
/	Slash delete. Messages ignored when 'slash delete' switch on the control unit console is activated. They are obeyed when switch is off.
%	Rewind stop
*	End of block

PROGRAMMING NOTES RELATING TO MILLING AND DRILLING EXERCISES

Pocket clearance cycle (G28) (see also p. 128)

1. Position the cutter over the centre point of the pocket.
2. Program the appropriate movement in the Z axis.
3. Program G28 with X and Y values indicating pocket dimensions. Cutter radius compensation and the step-over value will be automatically determined and implemented.
4. Cancel the cycle by programming G80.

Mirror image (G31) (see also p. 132)

1. Program G31 together with the axis or axes to be mirrored. For example, G31 *X* will mirror in the *X* axis only; G31 *XY* will mirror in the *X* and *Y* axes. No other data are to be included in this block.
2. Program the original axes commands.
3. Cancel by programming G30.

Cutter radius compensation (G41, G42) (see also p. 59)

1. Program G41 or G42 in the same block as G01 or G00 when making the approach move to the profile to be machined. The cutter will offset by the appropriate radius.
2. Cancel G41 or G42 by programming G40 in the withdrawal move.

Drill cycle (G81) (see also p. 124)

1. Program G81 with G00 when making the approach move to the first hole position. The block must also contain the *Z* depth to be drilled. The drill cycle will activate at the end of the positional move and will be repeated at the end of each subsequent positional move until cancelled.
2. Cancel G81 by programming G80 in the withdrawal move.

Peck drill cycle (G83) (see also p. 125)

1. Program G83 with G00 when making the approach move to the first hole position. The block must also contain the *Z* depth to be drilled and the peck distance as a *W* increment. The drill cycle will activate at the end of the positional move and will be repeated at the end of each subsequent positional move until cancelled.
2. Cancel G83 by programming G80 in the withdrawal move.

ALTERNATIVE MACHINE SPECIFICATION AND CONTROL SYSTEM FOR PROGRAMMING EXERCISES 9 TO 16: TURNING

Machine type and specification
Precision turning centre with two-axis control

Traverse: X transverse 160 mm (6.3 in.)
                                   Z longitudinal 450 mm (17.7 in.)
Spindle speed: 50–3800 rev/min
Feed: 0–400 mm/min
Tooling: Indexable turret providing eight tool stations

Control system
Program format: Word address
Axes controlled: X and Z singly or simultaneously
Interpolation: Linear X and Z axes
                                   Circular XZ plane
Command system: Absolute
Data input: MDI and magnetic tape

Programming information

Block numbers: N plus one to three digits
Preparatory functions: G plus two digits
  G00   Rapid traverse at machine maximum (modal)
  G01   Linear interpolation, programmed feed (modal)
  G02   Clockwise circular interpolation (modal)   } (see pp.
  G03   Counter-clockwise circular interpolation (modal) } 113–121)
  G08   Ramp down inhibit (modal) (see p. 122)
  G09   Cancels G08
  G33   Threading cycle (see p. 171)
  G40   Cutter offset cancel
  G41   Cutter radius compensation left (modal) (see p. 172)
  G42   Cutter radius compensation right (modal) (see p. 172)
  G70   Inch programming (modal)
  G71   Metric programming (modal)
  G80   Cancels all fixed cycles
  G81   Drill cycle (modal)   }
  G83   Peck drill cycle (modal)   } (see p. 172)
  G90   Absolute programming (modal)
  G91   Incremental programming (modal)
  G92   Feed in./min (modal)
  G93   Feed mm/min (modal)
  G94   Feed in./rev (modal)
  G95   Feed mm/rev (modal)
  G96   Surface cutting speed m/min
  G97   Surface speed ft/min
  G98   Spindle speed rev/min
Assigned miscellaneous functions: M plus two digits
  M00   Programmed stop. Stops all slide movement, spindle rotation and coolant.
  M01   Optional stop. Ignored unless activated manually from control console.

M02	End of program
M03	Clockwise spindle rotation
M04	Counter-clockwise spindle rotation
M05	Spindle off
M06	Tool change
M07	Coolant on (mist)
M08	Coolant on (flood)
M09	Coolant off
M30	End of program. Tape rewind.
Axis movement commands:	End point in X and Z
	Start point of arcs relative to circle centre I and K (see pp. 113–121)
	Dimensional values in 3/2 format, that is, three figures before and two after the decimal point. Program the decimal point but no leading or trailing zeros.
	Plus (+) signs are not required but (−) signs must be included.
	X values to be programmed as a diameter
Other functions:	
Feed	F plus four digits
	Feed/min in 1 mm or 0.1 in. steps
	Feed/rev in 0.001 mm or 0.001 in. steps
	Do not program decimal point
Spindle speed	S plus four digits
Surface speed	S plus three digits
Tool identity	T plus two digits, T01 to T10. With offsets plus four digits, offsets 00 to 24.
/	Slash delete. Messages ignored when 'slash delete' switch on the control unit console is activated. They are obeyed when switch is off.
%	Rewind stop
*	End of block

PROGRAMMING NOTES RELATING TO TURNING EXERCISES

Tooling system and turret indexing

The tooling system comprises an eight-station turret mounted at 90° to the machine spindle axis, the tooling positions being numbered 1 to 8. Figure 8.4 illustrates the way the tooling is arranged in relation to the workpiece.

Turret indexing is achieved as follows:

1. In the block following the end of a machining sequence program M06 (tool change). No other data are to be included in this block. The turret will withdraw to a pre-set safe indexing position.
2. In the next block program the required tool number and, if applicable, its related tool offset number. The turret will index by the shortest route to that tool position.
3. In the next block program a rapid move to the next pre-cutting position, which should be approximately 2 mm clear of the workpiece.
4. Finally, continue to program moves at a controlled feed rate.

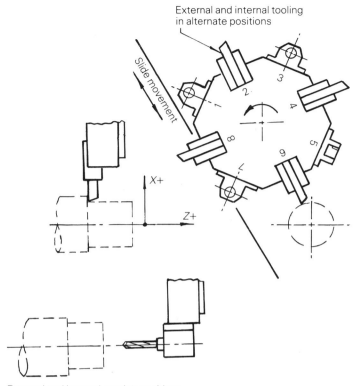

External and internal tooling
in alternate positions

External and internal turning positions

Figure 8.4   *Turret arrangement.*

Screw-cutting cycle (G33)

The movement sequence of the screw-cutting cycle is illustrated in Figure 8.5.

1. Tool moves rapidly to programmed *X* value.
2. Thread is cut to programmed *Z* value.
3. Rapid traverse to initial position in *X* axis.
4. Rapid traverse to initial position in *Z* axis.

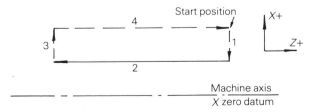

Figure 8.5

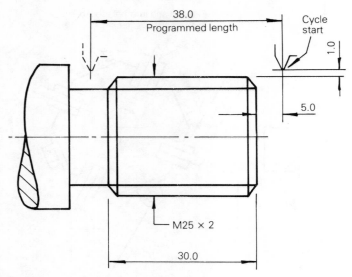

Figure 8.6 *Component detail.*

The final thread depth is reached by a series of passing cuts as indicated in the part program below, which refers to Figure 8.6.

The pitch is programmed as a *K* value.

Allow an approach distance of 5 mm in the *Z* axis and reduce the cutting speed to approximately two-thirds of the plain turning speed.

N	G	X	Z	I	K	F	S	T	M	*
–										
–										
–										
35	0	26.	5.							*
40	33	24.8	–38.		2		90	0404		*
45		24.6								*
50		24.4								*
55		24.2								*
60		24.								*
65		23.8								*
70		23.6								*

The *X* values are continually reduced until the full thread depth is reached. Two passes of the final cut should be made for finishing.

The *Z* axis move is programmed as an incremental value from the start position.

The cycle is cancelled by programming G80.

Drill cycles (G81 and G83) (see also pp. 124, 125)
1. Position drill at start point in the *Z* axis on *X* zero datum.

2. Program G81 or G83 together with *Z* depth to br drilled. G83 requires the peck distance to be programmed as a *W* increment.
3. Cancel G81 or G83 by programming G80.

Cutter radius compensation (G41 and G42)

Common to both turning and milling exercises. See p. 168.

PARTIALLY COMPLETED EXERCISES USING ALTERNATIVE CONTROL SYSTEMS

Exercise 1

PART PROGRAM EXERCISE NO. 1   MACHINE: As book   COMPILED BY: A. Programmer   CONTROL: As book   DATE: 28-3-84

N	G	X	Y	Z	I	J	K	%	F	S	T	M	*	REMARKS
01													*	Rewind stop
05	71												*	Metric units
10	90												*	Absolute
15	93												*	Feed mm/min
20	97												*	Speed rev/min
25	00	8000	4500	0									*	Rapid to Z0/P1
30										2000		03		Spindle/coolant on
35	01			-500					200		0101	08	*	Feed to Z depth
40	00		1300	0									*	Rapid to Z0
45	01			-500									*	Rapid to P2
50	00			0									*	Feed to Z depth
55		4000											*	Rapid to Z0
60	01			-500									*	Rapid to P3
65	00			0									*	Feed to Z depth
70			3000	0									*	Rapid to Z0
75	01			-500									*	Rapid to P4
80	00			0									*	Feed to Z depth
85			4500	-500									*	Rapid to Z0
90	01			0									*	Rapid to P5
95	00			0									*	Feed to Z depth
100		0	0	20000								00	*	Rapid to Z0

(Manual tool change)

Rapid to base datum
Program restart

Exercise 2

PART PROGRAM EXERCISE NO. 2 — MACHINE As book — CONTROL As book
COMPILED BY A.Programmer — DATE 8-5-84

N	G	X	Y	Z	I	J	K	F	S	T	M	*	REMARKS
01							%					*	Rewind stop
02	71											**	Metric units
03	91											*	Incremental
04	93											*	Feed mm/min
05	97											*	Speed rev/min
06	00	6000	-1500									*	Rapid to P1/2O
07									750		03		Spindle/coolant on
08	01			-1000				225		0101	07	*	Feed to Z depth
							D20				10	*	Dwell, Quill clamp
09			-4500									*	Feed in Y axis
10		2500										*	Feed in X axis
11			4500									*	Feed in Y axis
12											11	*	Quill clamp off
13	00			20000								*	Rapid lift
											00	*	Program stop

(Manual tool change)

Exercise 9

PART PROGRAM EXERCISE NO. 9								MACHINE As book		COMPILED BY A. Programmer		CONTROL As book DATE 20-6-84	
N	G	X	Y	Z	I	J	K	F	S	T	M	*	REMARKS
01								%				*	Rewind stop
05	71											*	Metric units
10	95											*	Feed mm/rev.
15	90											*	Absolute
20												*	Speed rev/min.
25										0202		*	Tool/offset
30	00	51·		0								*	Rapid to start
									2300		03		Spindle coolant on
35	01	0						300			07	*	Feed to X0
40	00			1·								*	Clear face
45		45·										*	Return in X axis
50	01			-78·					1275			*	Feed in Z axis
55	00	46·										*	Clear diam.
60				1·								*	Return to start
65		40·										*	Rapid in X axis
70	01			-55·					1432			*	Feed in Z axis
75	00	41·										*	Clear diam.
80				1·								*	Return to start
85		35·										*	Rapid in X axis
90	01			-55·					1637			*	Feed in Z axis
95	00	36·										*	Clear diam.
100				1·								*	Return to start

Exercise 10

PART PROGRAM / EXERCISE NO.	MACHINE	COMPILED BY	CONTROL	DATE
10	As book	A. Programmer	As book	5-6-84

N	G	X	Y	Z	I	J	K	F	S	T	M	*	REMARKS
01							%					*	Rewind stop
05	71											*	Metric
10	95											*	Feed mm/rev.
15	96											*	Speed m/min.
20										0202		*	Tool and offset
25	00	104.		0								*	Rapid to start
30											03	*	Spindle/coolant on
35	01	0							250/170		08	*	Feed to X0
40	00			2.								*	Clear face
45											06	*	Tool change
50										0101		*	Index to c/drill
55	00	0		2.								*	Rapid to start
60	01			-5.				80	28			*	Centre drill
65	00			2.								*	Return to start
70											06	*	Tool change
75										0303		*	Index to drill ⌀10
80	00	0		2.								*	Rapid to start
85	83			-85.			w20180					*	Peck drill ⌀10
90	80											*	Cancel cycle
95											06	*	Tool change
100										0505		*	Index to drill ⌀20
105	00	0		2.								*	Rapid to start
110	81			-85.				300				*	Drill ⌀20

9

ADVANCED TECHNIQUES

CAD/CAM: COMPUTER-AIDED DESIGN AND MANUFACTURE

The expression 'computer-aided design', or more commonly the abbreviation CAD, is the term used to describe the process by which engineering designers use the computer as a creative tool allowing them to produce, evaluate, modify and finalise their designs. The computer becomes a terminal at which the designer sits to analyse data, make calculations and use the computer graphics to build up quickly and efficiently a three-dimensional image of a projected design. The image can be rotated and viewed from different angles, sectioned through various planes, stretched, condensed and generally assessed. Modifications can be made instantly. As each stage of the design process proceeds the resulting data can be stored and retrieved at will, the computer's storage capacity providing, as one equipment manufacturer's advertisement stated, 'a drawing board as big as Wembley Stadium'.

When the designer is satisfied the details of the design can be transferred to a second terminal which is, in effect, a drafting or drawing station. Here the draftsman or draftswoman transforms the original designs into a series of engineering drawings which he or she creates on the computer screen, and again at this stage each individual component can be rotated, sectioned, scaled up or down and so on in a further process of evaluation which may or may not result in modifications to the original design. When this task is finished, fully dimensioned drawings can be printed from an interfaced printer or plotter, or alternatively the information can be stored as numerical data for later retrieval.

Computer-aided manufacture, CAM, is the term generally used to describe manufacturing processes that are computer controlled. One very important manufacturing process is metal cutting, and the computer involvement in this area of activity has been the subject of this text. Metal cutting is, however, just one type of manufacturing process that is computer controlled. There are many others: welding, flame cutting, presswork, electro-discharge machining, parts assembly, and so on.

177

All the processes listed above are truly manufacturing processes, that is, the end result is a component or an assembly of components. But there are a host of other essential functions that play a part in the overall set-up. The supply of materials and tooling, part programming and process control are some functions which are workshop-related. Spreading the net further, there are the financial aspects—marketing, stock control and distribution, for example—and of course there is the design and drafting process discussed earlier. It is possible for all these functions to be interrelated via computer control into a total computerised manufacturing system.

Since it is the practical aspects of the system that are most likely to be of interest to the reader, that is, the design and making of the product, the relationships between these two areas are worthy of further comment and are perhaps the key elements in the system. In the past, CAD and CAM, that is the production element of CAM, have developed as two separate activities, with the application of computers to the production process being somewhat ahead of CAD. Increasingly, even in small companies, they are now being seen not as two related functions but as one integrated function. Already the more sophisticated design/drafting systems are linked to the manufacturing process via part-programming facilities. Manufacturing aspects are fully considered at the design stage, and machine-control tapes are produced direct from design data rather than from a separate, and therefore error prone, analysis of an already finalised engineering drawing. The process may also, ultimately, eliminate the need for conventional drawings. Total numerical engineering has arrived, and the rate at which it is implemented especially in large companies is likely to be rapid.

COMPUTER-AIDED PART PROGRAMMING

When a program is compiled for a numerically controlled machining operation the programmer has to define machine movements in numerical terms that will result in the correct cutter path necessary to produce the desired component shape. With a good many components, particularly those requiring straight-line moves, this is a relatively simple task, but from time to time a programmer may be confronted with a component where the cutter path is less easy to define. This situation is more likely to occur where drawings are still dimensioned without regard to the numerically controlled machining process.

Consider the component shown in Figure 9.1. The method used to dimension the component is traditional and for production by conventional means would be perfectly acceptable. But to write a program for numerical control the programmer needs to know the co-ordinates of the arc centre, together with dimensional data relating to the start and finish points of the curve. Calculations have to be made before the programmer can proceed.

The calculations for the above example are not too involved and can quite

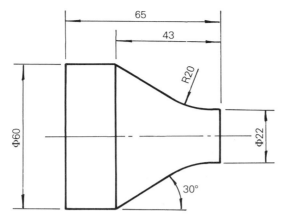

Figure 9.1 *Conventional dimensioning.*

easily be done on a pocket calculator. It is when the machined profile is very complex that computing facilities may be an advantage.

Early computer-aided programming involved the use of a general-purpose processor and a specially developed programming system called APT (automatically programmed tools). APT enabled the programmer to define the work profile as a series of interrelated points, lines and curves using a unique form of pidgin English. This was done by the programmer imagining himself or herself in a position above the cutting tool and then directing it by a series of statements along the required path. From the input of these statements the computer would make all the necessary calculations, including making an allowance for the cutter diameter to be used, and produce data that defined the appropriate tool path. These data would then need to be translated, via a post processor, into a form acceptable to the individual machine control unit so that it could be included in the part program.

Over the years there have been many developments in the computer-aided programming field and today there are a number of systems that cater for two-dimensional profiles in a very simple way. No special computer-programming knowledge is necessary, and the manufacturers of these systems claim that the ability to read an engineering drawing is all that is required.

The use of these systems is often referred to as 'geometric part programming', since they involve defining the profile by its geometric shape. The precise way in which the profile is defined varies from system to system. One method involves breaking the profile down into a series of intersecting points as illustrated in Figure 9.2. Once the profile has been defined in this way the dimensional position of each point in relation to a given datum and, where necessary, additional information as to whether the point is to be reached by angular or radial movement, is fed into the computer. Then, using the special language, the complete machining program is developed. Each profile feature

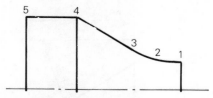

Figure 9.2 *Definition of a profile as a series of intersecting points.*

is called by the minimum of input data and the computer carries out all the necessary calculations to produce the required tool movement.

Programming systems of this type also incorporate canned cycles for roughing, screw cutting, etc., and speeds and feeds are often selected automatically following data input related to stock material, surface finish and tooling files retained within the computer.

GRAPHICAL NUMERICAL CONTROL

Graphical numerical control is the term used to describe the various ways in which computer graphics are used as an aid to part programming. One such method was mentioned in Chapter 5, when the use of computer graphics as an aid to program proving was discussed.

Computer graphics may also be used as part of the program-writing processes either to verify data as they are entered or to determine data.

In order to verify data input the computer, which may be the dedicated computer of the machine control unit or an off-machine programming station, is first programmed with data defining the area in which machining can safely take place. This is followed by an input of data defining the blank size from which the component is to be made. The safe machining area and the blank, suitably positioned, are displayed on the computer screen. The machine program is then entered and as each data entry is made the tool path will be indicated, thus giving visual confirmation that the entry is valid. It is possible to enlarge areas of a program for a more detailed examination of the cutter path if this should be desired. On completion of the program entry a rapid re-run is possible for further confirmation of the accuracy of the data entry before a final commitment to machining is made.

In order to use computer graphics to determine data, the profile to be machined is first defined geometrically in a manner similar to that employed for geometric programming. The shape thus defined is then displayed on the visual display unit. The cutter to be used to machine the component is represented by a circle which also appears on the screen and can be caused to move about by push-button control, thus simulating the desired cutter path.

To machine a profile or clear a pocket, for example, the cutter is brought to its starting position, which is recorded, via a data transfer button, as a positive feature of the machine program. The cutter is then moved to its next position and this too is transferred to the machine program. Further moves are made, perhaps on a trial-and-error basis, to determine the most appropriate, and each time the final position of the cutter is transferred to the machine program, the process continuing until machining is complete. On completion the series of moves can be re-run to check their validity and then supplemented by additional data such as feed rates, cutting speed and so on to complete the part program.

Another system simply involves moving a flashing cursor from one point to the next on the graphic image. The computer, acting on data relating to metal-removal rates which are already stored in the memory, then determines appropriate tool paths, indicates them visually in relation to the component profile and includes them in the part program. This technique is referred to as automatic programming.

Data developed by graphical means can be transferred to magnetic tape, disc or perforated tape for storage or transmission.

PARAMETRIC PROGRAMMING

A parameter is a quantity which is constant in one particular case but variable in others. A simple engineering example of a parameter is the length of a bolt. One version of the bolt will have a certain length; all other versions will be identical, that is, they will have the same thread form, diameter and hexagon head, but they will all vary in length. Thus the length of the bolt is a parameter, constant in one particular case but variable in others.

Parametric programming involves defining parameters and then using those parameters as the basis for one part program that may be used to machine not only the original component but a number of variations as well.

Figure 9.3(a) shows a component the dimensional features of which have been defined as parameters using the symbol # and a number: #1, #2, #3 and so on.

Figures 9.3(b) to 9.3(g) shows six variations of the component, the variations being indicated. A range of components such as this is referred to as a family of parts.

The machine movements necessary to machine each of the variations are all included in the original component. Some components require exactly the same movements, but with varying lengths of travel. Other components do not require all of the movements to be made. Using the more usual programming techniques, the production of each component would require a separate part program. Using the parametric part programming technique, instead of defining each dimensional movement individually in the X and Z axes, the paramet-

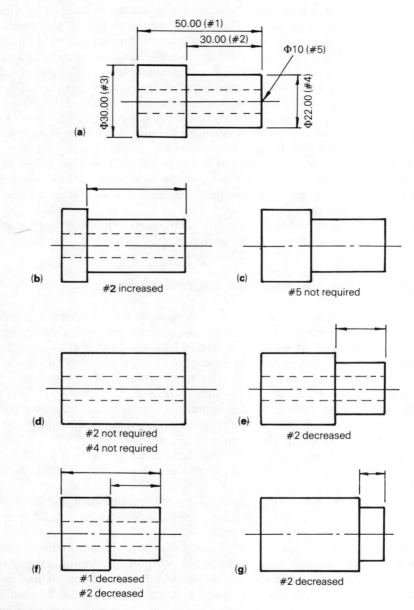

Figure 9.3 A 'family of parts'.

ric reference is programmed. Thus, to turn along the stepped diameter, the entry in the main program, sometimes referred to as the 'macro body', would read as follows:

$$N07 \quad G01 \quad X\#4 \quad Z\#2$$

This entry would suffice for all components requiring a stepped diameter. Equally, one entry using parametric identification would suffice for facing all the components to length or drilling the hole.

Having programmed all movements and the sequence in which they are to occur, it remains to dimensionally define them. The dimensional details are entered as a list at the start of the part program. Thus the parameters and their dimensional values for the original components would read as follows:

$$\#1 = 50.00$$
$$\#2 = 30.00$$
$$\#3 = 30.00$$
$$\#4 = 22.00$$
$$\#5 = 10.00$$

As each parameter is called in the macro body the programmed dimensional entry made previously will be invoked.

To machine any of the variations in the family of parts requires a simple amendment of the original parametric values. The parameters to machine the component shown in Figure 9.3(b) would be:

$$\#1 = 50.00$$
$$\#2 = 40.00 \text{ (amended)}$$
$$\#3 = 30.00$$
$$\#4 = 22.00$$
$$\#5 = 10.00$$

and to machine the component in Figure 9.3(f):

$$\#1 = 40.00 \text{ (amended)}$$
$$\#2 = 20.00$$
$$\#3 = 30.00$$
$$\#4 = 22.00$$
$$\#5 = 10.00$$

Now consider the components where the programmed movements necessary for machining the basic component are not required. By using a relatively simple programming technique the control unit can be caused to skip the redundant blocks. The necessary program entry involves the use of certain conditional expressions in which assigned abbreviations are used, such as the following:

EQ = equal to
NE = not equal to
GT = greater than
LT = less than
GE = greater than or equal to
LE = less than or equal to

Consider Figure 9.3(d) and assume the #1 and #3 have been machined. In the macro body the next call will be to machine the stepped diameter. To avoid this, blocks must be slipped and so an entry in the macro body will read as follows:

N15 IF [#4 EQ 0] GO TO N18

This statement says that if #4 is zero, move on to block number 18. Since #4 is non-existent in the component, the parametric value will be entered as zero and consequently the control unit will move ahead.

The above description of the use of the parametric programming technique is a very simple one. It is in fact a very powerful concept and its full application quite complex. For instance, parameters may be mathematically related within the macro body, that is, they may be added together, subtracted from one another, and so on.

In addition, the parametric principle may be extended to include speeds and feeds, when all the likely variations for roughing, finishing, etc. may be given a parametric identity and called into the macro body as and when required. It is applicable to the normal range of machining activity.

DIGITISING

Digitising is the name given to a technique used to obtain numerical data direct from a drawing or model. To obtain numerical data from a drawing, which may or may not be dimensioned, it is placed on a special tablet, or table, and a probe or ballpoint pen is traced over the drawing outline. This movement is received by a computer and is transformed into digital or dimensional values. Only two-dimensional data can be obtained from a drawing. For three-dimensional data a model of the component is required, and a probe which is electronic in operation is traced over the surface of the model, this movement being recorded by the computer as before.

Numerical data obtained by digitising can be used as the basis of a numerical control program. The technique is only suitable for certain types of machining, such as profile milling, but the concept is likely to be developed to cater for a wider range of machine-shop activity.

FLEXIBLE MANUFACTURING SYSTEM

A flexible manufacturing system (FMS) is a computer-controlled machining arrangement which will cater for a variety of continuous metal-cutting operations on a range of components without manual intervention. The objective of such a system is to produce components at the lowest possible cost, and in particular components that are required only in small quantities. Thus a prime requirement of such a system is flexibility, that is, the capacity to switch from one type of component to another, or from one type of machining to another, without interruption in the production process.

Production costs per unit item decrease as the number of components required increases. Large production runs justify extensive capital expenditure on special-purpose machinery that does a particular job very efficiently and quickly. Machines of this type, however, are rarely adaptable to other types of work: they lack flexibility. When flexibility does exist—one skilled worker and one machine, for instance, where single components can be handled in random order—the production rate is slow and therefore costly. Modern flexible manufacturing systems aim to bridge the gap between these two extremes.

Flexible manufacturing systems have been made possible by the fact that modern machine control units can store in the computer memory a number of part programs which can be activated via a master computer program in random order, a system referred to as direct numerical control (DNC). The same master computer is also able to control the supply of workpieces to the machine. The third important factor, tooling, will be controlled by the part program itself, but if a wide range of machining is to be carried out the tooling magazine will be required to accommodate a large number of tools; for milling operations at least 60 and perhaps more than 100 may be necessary.

A flexible manufacturing system will include at least two machines. When just two or three machines are involved the arrangement is sometimes referred to as a 'machining cell'. A fully integrated system will include more machines than this and they will vary in type. Figure 9.4 illustrates the principle. Installations of this nature are, of course, very costly and not in common use at present. However, the modular approach to building such a system, that is, starting with two machines and then adding additional machines as and when investment funds are available, would suggest that the concept is set to become a dominant feature of machine-shop engineering.

The automatic supply of work to each machine is an essential feature of any system, big or small. The use of pallets is the most favoured method, particularly for machining centres as opposed to turning centres, although they are also used for turning work. When pallets are used for turning work the final loading of the machine usually involves a robot. Figure 9.5 shows how one robot may be positioned to service two machines.

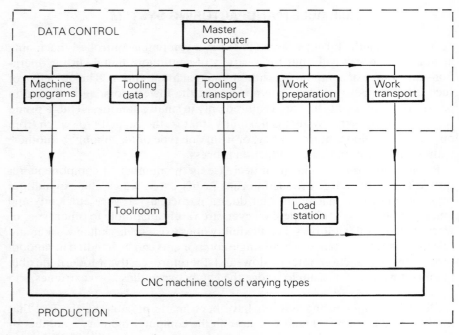

Figure 9.4   *Computerised control of a manufacturing system.*

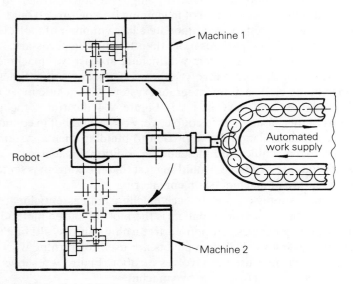

Figure 9.5   *Robot loading of turning centres.*

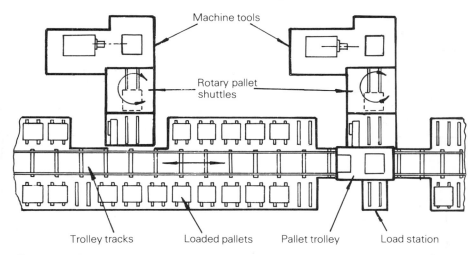

Figure 9.6 *Flexible manufacturing system using racked palletised work supply.*

The way pallets are used for milling operations will vary according to the type of work being handled and the space available. Figure 9.6 illustrates the use of a rack. Such a system as this is relatively simple and capable of modification and extension as and when required. More complex systems involve the use of pallet trolleys moving about the factory along predetermined routes, guided by inductive control wires buried in the workshop floor. Each machine will have its own load/unload station and there will be a master load/unload station to which each trolley returns at the end of a journey. Figure 9.7 illustrates the principle. Yet another approach is to use trolleys running along rails.

Pallets may be fed to the machines in a predetermined order which means their positioning in the work queue is critical, otherwise a workpiece may be subjected to the wrong machining cycle! Alternatively, they may be fed to the machine in random order and identified, usually by a photo-electric device responding to a number card attached to the pallet, when they arrive at the machine. On being identified the correct machining program for that workpiece will be called.

The preparation of work pallets is generally a manual operation. Their positioning and clamping in the machine are totally automated and, as a result, monitoring of their installation is necessary before machining commences. Limit switches are a common feature of such control, and one method involving a combination of pneumatic and electrical principles is illustrated in Figure 9.8.

Mention was made earlier of the high cost of flexible manufacturing systems which has, to date, limited their introduction. An intermediate approach to total automation is the use of automatic pallet-loaders dedicated to one machine. The pallet pool may be rectangular, oval or round and when fully

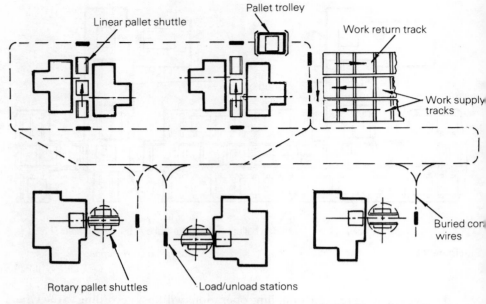

Figure 9.7 *Flexible manufacturing system using remote controlled trolley work supply.*

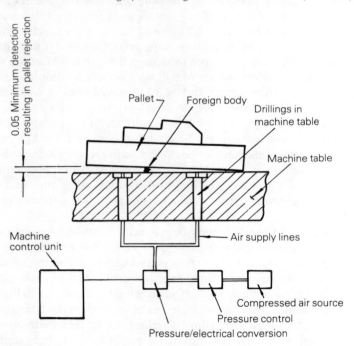

Figure 9.8 *Pallet location control.*

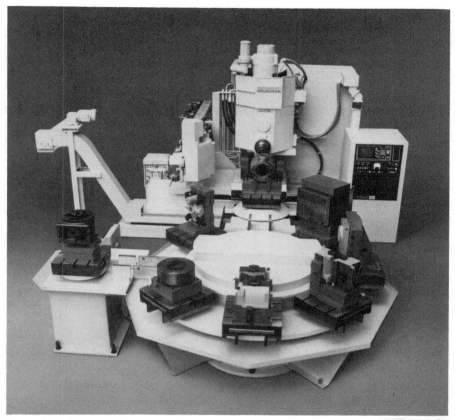

Figure 9.9 *Processing centre providing unmanned production runs.*

loaded will provide for an extended unsupervised production run lasting several hours, perhaps overnight or throughout a weekend. Figure 9.9 illustrates such an arrangement, referred to as a 'processing centre' by the manufacturers; its flexibility is indicated by the range of components shown in position on the pallets. Figure 9.10 shows a robot-loaded turning centre where work chutes provide a similar capability.

ADAPTIVE CONTROL

Adaptive control is the term used to describe the facility which enables a machine control unit to recognise certain variations from the original conditions which may occur during a machining process, and to make a compensating response. Unless such a response is made the effect of the variations may be to damage the machine, tooling or workpiece. Adaptive control is basically a data

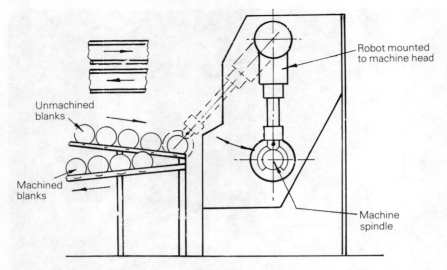

Unmachined blanks

Machined blanks

Robot mounted to machine head

Machine spindle

Figure 9.10 *Robot loading facility providing unmanned production runs on a turning centre.*

'feedback' rather like the closed-loop facility described in Chapter 1, which monitored slide positioning.

A number of unacceptable things can occur during a metal-cutting operation. For example, a tool may lose its cutting edge. On manually operated machines this would immediately be obvious to the operator, who would react accordingly. It is this type of response that adaptive control endeavours to emulate.

Now supposing the tool becomes blunt on an automatic machining process. What is the likely effect? At least three things are likely to occur. First, the power necessary to turn the machine spindle is likely to increase, that is, there would be a torque variation. Second, there is likely to be a build-up in temperature between the cutting tool and the workpiece, as the tool tends to rub rather than cut. Last, the tool itself is likely to deflect. By monitoring, that is measuring, these variations and taking corrective action damage can be averted.

Torque monitoring of spindle and servo motors is one method of adaptive control that is highly favoured. The power consumption is monitored electronically and the application of the technology involves programming the control unit with data that will define the maximum and minimum torque values permitted for any particular operation. Assume that during a metal-cutting sequence the maximum torque value at the cutting tool is reached, indicating perhaps that the tool is blunt or the component material is harder than anticipated. The control unit will respond to the feedback signal by lowering the feed rate and/or varying the spindle speed.

Consider another situation where, after modifications to feed and spindle speed, the torque continues to increase to a point where the spindle is

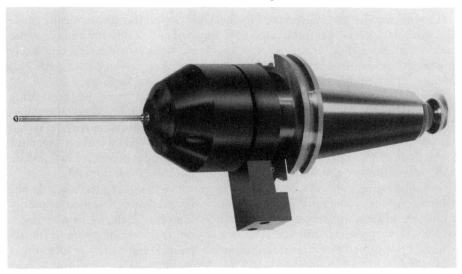

Figure 9.11 *Precision surface sensing probe.*

overloaded. In this case the control unit would inhibit the sequence and indicate a 'warning' signal on the visual display screen. The problem can then be investigated and the conditions rectified.

The torque monitoring feature can also be used to detect the minimum torque that is programmed to occur after a certain length of slide travel. If the programmed torque does not occur there may be two possible reasons. One is that the cutting tool is broken and has not made contact, a broken drill for example; the other is that the workpiece itself is not in position. Total inhibition of the machining process may be the necessary response, or alternatively a duplicate tool already in the magazine or turret could be called.

Torque monitoring taken to its extreme means that spindle speeds and feeds can be omitted from part programs. Provided the control unit is programmed with the values of the maximum permitted speeds and feed rates, it is possible for the adaptive control to adjust them to suit the prevailing cutting conditions. For instance, when the torque is high the feed would reduce, but when it is low, as for example when no cutting is taking place, the feed would be rapid.

Another approach to adaptive control is one which concerns itself with monitoring the presence of workpieces by the use of surface-sensing probes. Such a probe is illustrated in Figure 9.11 and is used in milling operations. The probe is mounted in the tool magazine alongside the cutting tools and can be called into operation via the part program, in the same way as a cutting tool, and be mounted in the machine spindle. The probe is electronic in operation and the stylus is interchangeable to accommodate different applications. It can be programmed to detect the presence, by touching on, of a surface in three axes and, if the surface is not present, it will inhibit the machining cycle.

Probes can also be programmed to check stock size and automatically cause the work datums to be offset to locate the finished part within the bounds of the stock material, thus ensuring that the final work surface is completely machined. If insufficient stock is present the machining is not performed. This facility is particularly useful when machining castings or forgings.

Another application of a probe is to speed up a cycle by preventing non-metal-cutting passes of the cutting tool. For example, when machining casting or forgings, the part program will need to cater for all possibilities and may well include passing cuts that will be necessary only when there is excessive stock to be removed. If the probe detects that no metal is present, the feed rate will automatically be maximised or a program block may be skipped.

An interesting method of detecting the presence of cutting tools is a device which combines pneumatic and electronic principles. It is designed primarily for use on machining centres to monitor small-diameter drills, taps and reamers which are very prone to break. The device is in the form of a simple caliper which is positioned at a convenient point on the machine bed. The location of the caliper is predetermined and after use the cutting tool is moved via the part program so that it positions within the caliper. When in position a jet of air is blown from one side of the caliper and if the cutting tool is missing this jet of air will blow on to a pressure-sensitive electrical device housed in the opposite arm of the caliper. This will generate a signal to the machine control unit which will result in either the machining process being halted or the tool being replaced in the program by a sister tool already housed in the magazine. If the tool is present then there will be no air flow between the two arms of the caliper and the tool will automatically be replaced in the tool magazine to await a further call. Figure 9.12 illustrates the technique.

Another method of detecting broken or blunt tooling involves the use of sound sensors. A cutting tool which is cutting properly will emit a certain sound. If the tool loses its edge or breaks, the sound it makes as it attempts to cut metal will be different from the original. The sound sensors detect the variation and will cause the program to be stopped or, alternatively, will call in a sister tool to replace the original.

Adaptive control is an area of computerised numerically controlled machining that is the subject of much research and experiment, and it is an area in which there are likely to be further very interesting developments.

IN-PROCESS MEASUREMENT

In-process measurement is the term used to describe the automatic measurement or gauging of a component while it is in position on the machine, and while the correction of errors is still possible. It is not a new concept. The need for automatic measurement went hand in hand with the development of automatic machining processes, and fully automated machines performing a variety of operations were around long before the advent of computerised numerical control.

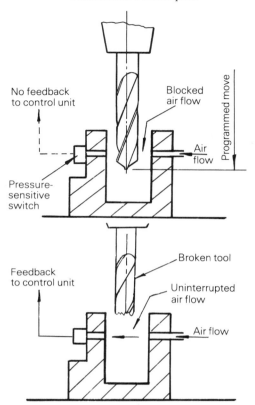

Figure 9.12 *Broken tool detection unit.*

In-process measurement presents many difficulties. A machining area, with its accumulation of swarf and coolant, is not an ideal place to carry out precision measurement involving delicate instruments or monitoring devices. Nevertheless, a number of very successful devices have been developed over the years, their method of operation being based on mechanical, pneumatic, optical and electronic principles.

Many of the earlier devices, though not all, were 'open loop', that is, there was no feedback of data to the machine controls and so there was no automatic adjustment of the machine setting to compensate for unacceptable size variations. Correction was possible only by manual intervention, but at least this was usually possible without halting the machining process.

On modern CNC machines the accuracy with which slide movements are generally made and monitored can, in the case of some classes of work, eliminate the need for further control, since the slide movements, and therefore the relative tool movements, are made to an accuracy which may well be within the dimensional tolerances of the component. In other cases this degree of

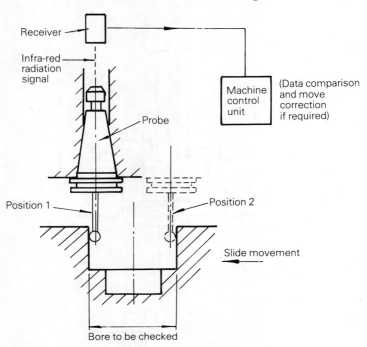

Figure 9.13   *In-process measurement by electronic probe.*

control is insufficient and, as was stated in Chapter 2, transducers which monitor slide movement or leadscrew rotation may not give an accurate indication of the tool and work relationship. For instance, a tool may wear, thus affecting the dimensional size of the component, but this will have no connection with slide movement and no compensation will be made. Similarly, the workpiece may not be precisely located, or may be impossible to locate precisely, so again some monitoring and correction of movement may be necessary to ensure that surfaces are relatively positioned. These are the sorts of situations that in-process measuring can monitor.

The modern in-process measuring device is electronic in operation. It consists of a probe, and is capable of monitoring positional variations in three axes. The way in which it is applied will depend on the machine type, but it can be applied to the measurement of internal and external diameters, lengths, depths of slots, hole centres, and so on. Programmed air blasts are used to clean the work prior to measurement.

One method of using touch sensors requires reference to be made to an established datum, which may be a surface which is part of the machine structure, for example a tailstock barrel, or a surface on the component. The program will bring the sensor into contact with the reference face and record its position as zero. It will then be moved to the surface being checked and the resulting move will be compared by the machine control unit with a pre-programmed value. If there is a variation a compensation in the relative tool offset will be made.

Features such as a bored hole diameter can be measured by touching on at each side of the hole, and the resulting movement, plus the stylus diameter of the probe, will indicate the hole size. The necessary calculation will be made by the control unit and again a comparison will be made with a pre-programmed value and tool offsets initiated as required. The technique is illustrated in Figure 9.13.

Measurement of this nature is not completely divorced from the machine slide movement, and its accuracy can never be better than the resolution, that is, the smallest increment that can be determined by the control unit, of the machine.

The principle of varying tool offsets as a result of information fed back to the control system via a probe can be extended to include the setting of the original offset. It involves the probe touching the tools and comparing their position with a datum—the number 1 tool, for example—and setting the offsets accordingly, thus eliminating yet another aspect of manual intervention.

QUESTIONS

1   Describe two ways in which computer graphics are used as an aid to part programming.

2   Describe briefly the meaning of CAD/CAM.

3   What is a flexible manufacturing system?

4   What characteristic of computer technology makes the concept of FMS feasible?

5   What do you understand by the term 'in-process measurement'? Explain how it might be applied to checking the size of a turned diameter.

6   What is torque monitoring? State two instances where its application may be useful in an automated machining process.

7   How are sound sensors used to monitor cutting-tool condition?

8   What is a sister tool?

9   Describe the technique of digitising.

10 Describe parametric programming and explain the advantages of the technique.

ANSWERS TO CHAPTER 7

1   Surface cutting speed 170 m/min
     Spindle speed 984 rev/min

2   Spindle speed 2255 rev/min

3   607 per cent increase when using cemented carbide tools

5   Feed 0.15 mm/rev
     Surface cutting speed 170 m/min
     Spindle speed 1546 rev/min
     Feed 232 mm/min

6   Spindle speed 3979 rev/min

8   Feed 0.15 mm/tooth
     Feed 0.3 mm/rev
     Spindle speed 1592 rev/min
     Feed 477 mm/min

9   Spindle speed 796 rev/min

10   Feed 3.6 mm/rev

INDEX